JUDICIAL REVIEW IN SCOTLAND

JUDICIAL REVIEW IN SCOTLAND

Tom Mullen, Kathy Pick
and
Tony Prosser

School of Law,
University of Glasgow

JOHN WILEY & SONS
Chichester · New York · Brisbane · Toronto · Singapore

First published in the United Kingdom by John Wiley & Sons Ltd,
Baffins Lane, Chichester,
West Sussex PO19 1UD, England

National   01243 779777
International   (+44) 1243 779777

Copyright © 1996 by TJ Mullen

All rights reserved.

No part of this book may be reproduced by any means,
or transmitted, or translated into a machine language
without the written permission of the publisher.

Other Wiley Editorial Offices

John Wiley & Sons Inc., 605 Third Avenue,
New York, NY 10158-0012, USA

John Wiley & Sons, Inc., 7222 Commerce Center Drive,
Suite 240, Colorado Springs, CO 80919

Jacaranda Wiley Ltd, 33 Park Road, Milton,
Queensland 4064, Australia

John Wiley & Sons (Canada) Ltd, 22 Worcester Road,
Rexdale, Ontario M9W 1L1, Canada

John Wiley & Sons (Asia) Pte Ltd, 2 Clementi Loop #02–01,
Jin Xing Distripark, Singapore 0512

British Library Cataloguing Publication Data

A catalogue record for this book is available from the British Library

ISBN 0-471-96614-2

Typeset in 10/12pt Baskerville by Footnote Graphics, Warminster, Wilts
Printed and bound in Great Britain by Redwood Books, Trowbridge.

This book is printed on acid-free paper responsibly manufactured from sustainable forestation,
for which at least two trees are planted for each one used for paper production.

CONTENTS

	Page
FOREWORD	ix

Chapter 1
INTRODUCTION AND ACKNOWLEDGEMENTS — 1

Chapter 2
JUDICIAL REVIEW IN SCOTLAND: THE KEY CHARACTERISTICS AND RESEARCH ISSUES — 5

The development of judicial review procedure in Scotland	5
The Dunpark Report and the new procedure	7
The new procedure in practice	10
Key questions for research: use of judicial review	11
Key questions for research: the procedure	13

Chapter 3
THE USE OF JUDICIAL REVIEW — 17

The number of petitions	17
The subject-matter of judicial review petitions	18
Who seeks judicial review?	22
Against whom is judicial review sought?	27
Outcomes	29
Statutory review	36
Conclusions	38

Chapter 4
JUDICIAL REVIEW PROCEDURE — 41

The speed of judicial review	41

Effects of the lack of a leave filter	*46*
Expenses and legal aid	*47*
Use of nominated judges	*49*
Interim relief	*50*
Title and interest to sue	*52*
Competence	*54*
Damages	*55*
Conclusions	*55*

Chapter 5
LEGAL AID AND JUDICIAL REVIEW *57*

Introduction	*57*
The legal aid system	*59*
Number and distribution of legal aid applications	*64*
Speed of processing applications	*73*
Grant and refusal of legal aid applications	*75*
Solicitors' views on the grant and refusal of legal aid	*79*
The outcome of legally aided judicial reviews	*82*
Appropriateness of the reasonableness test in judicial review cases	*83*
Summary and conclusions	*84*

Chapter 6
SURVEY OF SOLICITORS AND LAY ADVISERS *87*

Introduction	*87*
Sources of solicitors' casework	*89*
Identifying cases as suitable for referral to solicitors	*91*
Reasons for non-referral	*96*
Improving referral	*98*
Casework profile	*101*
Legal aid	*103*
Costs	*108*
Settlement	*109*
Procedures and remedies	*109*
Counsel	*110*
Outcomes	*110*
Knowledge and training	*111*
Other factors	*111*
Conclusions	*111*

Chapter 7
THE IMPACT OF JUDICIAL REVIEW *113*

Introduction	*113*
Defining and assessing impact	*114*

Prior research on homelessness *116*
The legal framework *118*
Local Authority A *120*
Local Authority B *127*
Summary and conclusions *132*

Chapter 8
CONCLUSIONS *135*

FOREWORD

The Right Honourable The Lord Hope of Craighead
Lord President of the Court of Session

Judicial review, as it is known in Scotland today, is not new in concept. The supervisory jurisdiction of the Court of Session was developed by the judges long ago, to enable the court to provide a remedy which was not otherwise available. But it was not until the court reformed the procedure in 1985, to enable the jurisdiction to be exercised quickly, simply and at minimum cost, that its full potential in the modern context began to be realised. Greatly improved access to the court was the key which unlocked the door which, for many, had previously remained shut.

The new procedure has now been in use for 10 years, and there is clearly a strong case for taking stock of what has been achieved so far. It is right that the system should be carefully scrutinised, to see what lessons are to be learned, what needs to be corrected and in what way the procedure can be improved. The court must, of course, play its own part in this exercise. It can and does keep its own procedures under constant review, and the judicial review procedure is within this remit. But before the litigant reaches the court he or she has to pass through other hands. The availability of the procedure has to be explained, a decision has to be made as to whether or not to make use of it, and there may be a request for legal aid. Therefore, the contributions made by the legal advisers at all levels, and by the Scottish Legal Aid Board, are also important in the assessment of how the procedure is working and what changes should be made.

The initiatives which have been shown in this field by the School of Law at the University of Glasgow are particularly welcome in these circumstances. First, there was a research project, which subjected the procedure in the court to careful analysis, and extended also into those other areas of practice which affect access to the court. Now there is the book. This is welcome, as its publication will enable the results of the research to be presented to a wide audience. It contains a clear and well-presented account of the nature of the present system and the use which is being made of it. The equivalent procedure in

England and Wales and Northern Ireland has also been studied, as experience in those jurisdictions provides a useful touchstone for comparison. The merits and defects of the Scottish system are identified, and recommendations for change are made wherever this is seen to be necessary.

The fact that the new procedure in Scotland has been found, in general, to be working well and achieving its objects, is satisfactory. But this book should not be read as an exercise in self-congratulation. Its importance lies in the guidance it gives as to areas where there may be room for improvement. It is here that the lessons for the future success of the procedure are to be learned. I hope that all who read this excellent book will benefit from this important research project, so that the procedure will continue to develop to best advantage in the service of those who require access to it.

Edinburgh
December 1995

Chapter 1

INTRODUCTION AND ACKNOWLEDGEMENTS

This book is the result of a project carried out in the School of Law of the University of Glasgow which examined the operation of judicial review in Scotland. In the past, examinations of the way in which legal procedures actually work have been relatively rare, although they are now becoming more common. Perhaps such detailed empirical study of the way courts work carries its own justification, but there were a number of circumstances which, we considered, made this study particularly timely.

First, judicial review is of considerable, and growing, current importance. It is the remedy available to the citizen who wishes to challenge actions and decisions of government when no other procedure is available. South of the Border there have been a number of well-publicised and successful challenges to government in areas ranging from the penal system and criminal injuries compensation, to overseas development, and the number of cases brought has increased dramatically over the last few years. Much credit for the growth of the cases has been given to procedural reforms carried out in England in 1977 which simplified the procedure for judicial review. These developments have generally been welcomed by judges and by other commentators as an important contribution to the role of the courts in policing the actions of government.

In Scotland, there have been fewer high-profile cases, and the numbers of judicial review petitions brought have been much smaller, although, once again, there has been a considerable increase in the numbers. As we shall describe in Chapter 2, although judicial review has a long history in Scotland, it is only since 1985 that it has been genuinely accessible through a relatively simple procedure and, almost 10 years later, the time seemed ripe for considering how this procedure is working.

Thus, one aim of the research was a straightforward one of determining whether the procedure for judicial review introduced in 1985 has lived up to expectations in providing an accessible and quick route for challenging the legality of government.

The work was made more timely, however, by the fact that it has proved possible to incorporate a developed comparative dimension. As mentioned above, the judicial review procedure in England and Wales had been reformed (though in ways very different to Scotland) in 1977, and a detailed study has recently been published setting out the results of detailed empirical research.[1] Similar work was also being carried out in Northern Ireland.[2] The opportunity was thus given to compare the procedures in the three jurisdictions, and, in particular, that of Scotland with the larger jurisdiction of England and Wales, in order to gauge the effects of the different types of procedural reform and the different characteristics of the courts in each jurisdiction. The comparative aspects of the research were given extra force by the fact that some serious difficulties had been identified in the reformed English procedure. Delay had become a grave problem, with a large backlog of cases having developed. This removed one of the key justifications of the new procedure: that it is a speedy means of establishing the legality of public decisions. The research mentioned above suggested that the apparent 'explosion' in the number of judicial review cases was a misleading indicator of the role of the procedure; use of judicial review was dominated by the two areas of immigration and housing, with little use in other important areas of public administration. Finally, the research found major inconsistencies in patterns of judicial decision-making in the initial stage of the procedure, that of granting leave to proceed with the application (a stage with no direct counterpart in Scotland). All these characteristics of the English procedure created incentives to discover whether they were replicated in Scotland or whether the peculiar Scottish procedure had succeeded in avoiding the difficulties encountered south of the Border. Moreover, were there any ways in which judicial review is used for different purposes in Scotland from those in England and Wales?

It is, of course, important not to see court procedures in isolation. Just as important as the ease of using the procedure itself, is the question of the extent to which the 'gatekeepers' to the courts in the form of the legal aid authorities and advisers operate in such a way as to ensure that access to justice is made as easy as possible in appropriate cases. Thus, it was decided to examine the award of legal aid so far as to do so was compatible with statutory requirements of confidentiality; it was possible here, also, to use comparative data from England and Wales. In addition, legal and lay advisers were also interviewed in order to establish both their views on the operation of the procedure and their roles in securing that it is used in appropriate cases.

Finally, most accounts of judicial review end at the stage of the decision of the courts. Yet the whole question of the impact of judicial review is a fascinating one. Are administrators aware when they are making decisions of the legal

---

[1] M Sunkin, L Bridges and G. Mészáros, *Judicial Review in Perspective*, Public Law Project, 1993. A second edition has been published (Cavendish, 1996).
[2] B Hadfield and E Weaver, 'Trends in Judicial Review in Northern Ireland' [1993] *Public Law*, pp 12–16.

constraints which surround them? What effect do even successful challenges have in practice? This latter point is of particular importance given that the usual effect of a successful petition for judicial review is that the decision is returned to the administrator who must take it again, this time lawfully, so that success in court by no means guarantees an eventual favourable decision from the authorities. To study this in depth would require another research project, but some attempt was made to assess the impact of judicial review in the area of housing, and a summary of this will be included in this report.

Our examination of the way the procedure works in Scotland and the related comparisons are set out in Chapters 3 and 4, after an introduction to judicial review and to the key questions which we felt needed researching in Chapter 2. These chapters draw on a detailed analysis of court records in all judicial review proceedings commenced in the six years 1988–1993 supplemented with interviews of advocates, advisers and some court staff.

In Chapter 5 we examine legal aid and judicial review. The availability or otherwise of legal aid may represent an important filter in determining which cases are able to reach the courts. We had hoped to study individual cases at this stage, but the statutory requirements of confidentiality prevented this; instead, we proceeded by examination of statistical information provided by the Scottish Legal Aid Board and through interviews with officials and legal and lay advisers. The role of advisers is analysed through a number of interviews, the results of which are set out in Chapter 6. Finally, the limited study of the impact of judicial review was carried out through examining the effect of the procedure and of decisions reached through it in the area of homelessness in two local authorities, and this forms the basis for the impact study in Chapter 7.

We have reason to be grateful to a large number of institutions and individuals for making the research possible. It was funded mainly by a generous grant from the Leverhulme Trust, supplemented by funds from the University of Glasgow New Initiatives Fund and the University of Glasgow School of Law. We are also, of course, extremely grateful to the Lord President for somehow finding time to read the work in draft, to provide useful comments and to write the Foreword. In making the business of researching such a smooth one we must thank Mr Hugh Foley, the Principal Clerk of Session and Justiciary, Mr Thomas Thomson, the Deputy Principal Clerk and Keeper of the Rolls, Mr Ronnie Alexander, the Paper Keeper and, in the petition Department, Mr Donald Bruton, Mr David Fraser, Nicola Fraser, Mr George Marple and Ms Fiona Merrilees.

At the Scottish Legal Aid Board we must express our thanks to Ms Elizabeth Watson, the Director of Legal Services, Miss Eve Crowe and Mrs Gilian Parmakov. We are also extremely grateful to the advocates, solicitors and lay advisers who so generously gave their time to assist us in our work, and to the officers of local authorities, who must remain anonymous to preserve the anonymity of the authority.

Apart from the three researchers named as authors of this book, Lee Bridges of the Public Law Project in London has acted as consultant and has proved invaluable as a source of ideas and in the provision of comparative material. Morna Roberts has performed demanding technical tasks with great efficiency.

With so many acknowledgements it is even more necessary than usual to stress that only the authors bear responsibility for the content of this book.

Chapter 2

JUDICIAL REVIEW IN SCOTLAND: THE KEY CHARACTERISTICS AND RESEARCH ISSUES

As the previous chapter suggested, the study of judicial review in Scotland was designed to complement work being carried out in England and Wales and in Northern Ireland. However, in Scotland, judicial review has characteristics which are very different from those in the other UK jurisdictions, and this chapter will outline some of them. It is indeed these very differences which give this research much of its usefulness as it permits effective comparisons to be drawn.

The development of judicial review procedure in Scotland

The leading case of *West v Secretary of State for Scotland* 1992 SLT 636 made quite clear the distinction between substantive law and procedure in establishing the relationship between English and Scots cases concerning judicial review. Drawing on earlier caselaw, the Lord President accepted 'that no difference of substance exists between the laws of England and Scotland with regard to the grounds on which judicial review may be open …'.[1] Nevertheless, 'the origins and development of judicial review in the two countries are indeed different … the English approach appears to be to fasten not upon principle but upon remedies, whereas the Scottish approach is based essentially upon principle'.[2] Thus, on matters of procedure (including, crucially, the scope of the judicial review procedure) Scots law is distinctive and some account of its development should be given before discussing procedural details.

As in England, judicial review has a long history.[3] For example, in 1829 the House of Lords accepted that 'a jurisdiction is given in this case to the Court of

---
[1] At 644.
[2] At 648.
[3] For a summary, see the decision of Lord President in *West v Secretary of State for Scotland* (*op. cit.*) at 639–45.

Session, not to review the judgment on the merits, but to take care that the Court of Presbytery shall keep within the line of its duty, and conform to the provisions of the Act of Parliament. There is in the Court of Session in Scotland that superintending authority over inferior jurisdictions, which is requisite in all countries, for the purpose of confining those inferior jurisdictions within the bounds of their duty...'.[4] Development of the law of judicial review through employing the supervisory jurisdiction of the Court of Session continued throughout the nineteenth and early twentieth centuries.

The problem was, however, that the procedure used in the Court of Session was slow and cumbersome, and this limited the number of cases brought; as one commentator has noted, 'before 1985 ... it was uncommon for more than a handful of applications to be raised in any one year'.[5] In 1969, both the English and the Scottish Law Commissions had been asked to review remedies in judicial review; whilst the review in England resulted in important reforms, that in Scotland never produced a report. Impetus for reform, however, came from the introduction in 1977 of the simplified English procedure under the new Order 53 of the Rules of the Supreme Court based on the (English) Law Commission's recommendations and from judicial pronouncements in cases concerning homelessness. A number of attempts had been made to challenge the decisions of housing authorities under the Housing (Homeless Persons) Act 1977 in the Sheriff Court. However, in *Brown v Hamilton District Council* 1983 SLT 397 the House of Lords held that the jurisdiction to review administrative action was exclusive to the Court of Session. Lord Fraser observed that 'it is for consideration whether there might not be advantages in developing special procedure in Scotland for dealing with questions in the public law area, comparable to the English prerogative orders ... [which] have advantages over ordinary procedures such as declaration, particularly by making available remedies which are speedy and cheap and which protect public authorities from unreasonable actions...'.[6] He reiterated this call for reform in *Stevenson v Midlothian District Council* 1983 SLT 433.[7] After requests to provide a statutory right of appeal to the Sheriff Court in homelessness cases, the Solicitor General announced instead that after consultation with the Lord Advocate a working party would be set up by the Lord President to recommend a simple form of procedure for judicial review. The Committee was established in 1983, chaired by Lord Dunpark, and reported in 1984.[8] The proposals were implemented (with some significant differences from the Committee's recommendations) from 30 April 1985 in the new rule of court 260B; with consolidation of the Rules of Court, the procedure is now contained in rule 58.[9]

---

[4] *Campbell v Brown* (1829) 3 W & S 441 at 448 (per Lord Lyndhurst LC).
[5] Page, 'Judicial Review in the Court of Session', in *Socio-Legal Research in the Scottish Courts Volume 2*, Scottish Office Central Research Unit papers, 55 at 58.
[6] At 418.
[7] At 437.
[8] *Report to the Rt Hon Lord Emslie, Lord President of the Court of Session, by the Working Party on Procedure for Judicial Review of Administrative Action* (1984).
[9] RCS 1965, r 260B, inserted by SI 1985 No 500 (now RCS, r 58).

The Dunpark Report and the new procedure

It is important to note that the Dunpark Report had the objective of developing a suitable procedure without the need to wait for Parliamentary legislation; instead, the changes were to be brought into operation by Act of Sederunt. This limited the scope of reform in one important respect: the Committee considered that the rules relating to title and interest to sue ('standing' in the usual English terminology) could not competently be changed in this way as they are rules of substantive law. Nevertheless, the Committee favoured the extension of standing through the adoption of the test 'sufficient interest': '[t]here is, in our opinion, a strong case for the extension by the legislature of our common law rules of title to sue to enable every person who is directly or indirectly affected by alleged unlawful acts or decisions competently to challenge them'.[10] No such legislative reform has been made.

The key principle adopted by the Dunpark Committee was to maximise flexibility in the new procedure through maximising control by the judge: 'we consider that the Judge must have power to grant any decree or make any order which he considers necessary or reasonable in the interests of justice. We think it important that every possible remedy should be made available in this process so that no ancillary litigation should be necessary. We have given the Judge complete control of the procedure so that he may at every stage assess the amount of time likely to be required by the parties before the next stage is reached'.[11] This resulted in some striking differences from the English procedure. Thus, in England a complex system of time limits was introduced, with applications having to be made promptly or, in any event, within three months of the decision; a decision filed even within three months may still be held to be out of time.[12] Not only is this far stricter than the time limit for most civil actions of at least three years, but the bad drafting of the relevant rules and statute have led to uncertainty and unnecessary litigation. By contrast, the Dunpark Committee rejected the imposition of a time limit as it believed that this would prevent the procedure being made exclusive. Instead, procedure is under control of the judge and delay in bringing the petition may affect the willingness of the court to grant a remedy.[13]

Secondly, a fundamental control over the procedure in England is the requirement that leave be obtained (usually *ex parte*) from the court before the case can progress to a full hearing. This has been the most heavily criticised aspect of the procedure in recent work, which has concluded that '[a]lthough it

---

[10] *Op. cit.* para 8.
[11] *Op. cit.* para 5.
[12] See Supreme Court Act 1981, s 31(6) and RSC Ord 53, r 4(1); *R v the Independent Television Commission ex parte TVNI Ltd* [1993] 2 FLR 886; *R v Dairy Produce Quota Tribunal ex parte Caswell* [1990] 2 AC 738.
[13] See *e.g. Hanlon v Traffic Commissioner* 1988 SLT 802; *Carlton v Glasgow Caledonian University* 1994 SLT 549.

is clear from the data that leave is a significant filter, the evidence indicates that there is a substantial risk that potentially arguable applications are being prematurely rejected. In particular, our data have highlighted both the uncertain nature of the leave hurdle and the considerable variation in approach amongst the judges'.[14] The requirement that leave be obtained was also rejected by the Dunpark Committee, which preferred that the judge should have power to dismiss an application as incompetent or irrelevant at a Preliminary Diet. The procedure actually adopted is that petitions are initially brought before a judge (usually *ex parte*) to deal with matters such as intimation and service and interim relief through the granting of a first order.[15] This does not, however, normally involve a substantive assessment of the merits (except by agreement) as does the leave decision south of the Border, although the court does have power to dismiss the petition at this stage, and, in immigration cases at least, the respondent may, in practice, oppose the application.[16] The case then proceeds to a first hearing at which the majority of petitions are determined.

A further matter on which there has been massive confusion and a great deal of procedural litigation in England is that of the scope of the judicial review procedure. To summarise briefly, the English procedure was not made exclusive in the sense that it had to be employed for all challenges to public bodies or all proceedings involving matters of public law. Nevertheless, the House of Lords held, in *O'Reilly v Mackman* [1983] 2 AC 237, that it was obligatory to use the procedure where a challenge was based on rights entitled to protection under public law; otherwise, public authorities would lose the protection of the time limit, the leave requirement and other specialities of the judicial review procedure. This spawned both complex caselaw and academic controversy, especially in view of the difficulty of importing distinctions between public and private law rights into a common law jurisdiction, although it appears that a somewhat more relaxed view is now being taken by the House of Lords which has permitted the use of procedures other than judicial review where an assertion of a private law right involves the determination of matter of public law.[17]

The Dunpark Committee recommended that the new procedure be exclusive in the sense that it was to be used for all applications for the exercise of the supervisory jurisdiction of the Court of Session. It also recommended that statutory review under the Acquisition of Land (Authorisation Procedure) (Scotland) Act 1947 (validity of compulsory purchase orders), the Special Roads Act 1949 (now the Roads (Scotland) Act 1984 (validity of orders)), and the Town and Country Planning (Scotland) Act 1972 (validity of structure plans and other orders) be brought within the new procedure, but with the retention of the special statutory time limit of six weeks. The first recommendation was

---

[14] M Sunkin, L Bridges and G Mészáros, *Judicial Review in Perspective*, Public Law Project, 1993, p 102; see also A LeSueur and M Sunkin, 'Applications for Judicial Review: The Requirement of Leave' [1992] *Public Law*, pp 102–129.
[15] RCS, 58.7.
[16] See *Butt v Secretary of State for the Home Department* 1995 GWD 16–905.
[17] *Roy v Kensington and Chelsea and Westminster Family Practitioner Committee* [1992] 1 AC 624.

2 THE KEY CHARACTERISTICS AND RESEARCH ISSUES

implemented in the new procedure, which specifies that applications to the supervisory jurisdiction *shall* be made by petition for judicial review. This has not avoided the difficulties experienced in England entirely, because at one stage the Court of Session appeared to follow English caselaw in defining the supervisory jurisdiction as depending on whether a matter of public law was raised in the application.[18] This approach was wholeheartedly repudiated by the First Division in *West v Secretary of State for Scotland* 1992 SLT 636, in which it held that the supervisory jurisdiction did not depend on any distinction between public and private law, but was available in relation to any decision-maker to whom a jurisdiction had been delegated or entrusted. The test was thus whether a 'tripartite relationship' existed which distinguished the situation from that of contractual rights and obligations. In the words of the court:

> (1) The Court of Session has power, in the exercise of its supervisory jurisdiction, to regulate the process by which decisions are taken by any person or body to whom a jurisdiction, power or authority has been delegated or entrusted by statute, agreement or any other instrument.
> (2) The sole purpose for which the supervisory jurisdiction may be exercised is to ensure that the person or body does not exceed or abuse that jurisdiction, power or authority or fail to do what the jurisdiction, power or authority requires.
> (3) The competency of the application does not depend upon any distinction between public law and private law, nor is it confined to those cases which English law has accepted as amenable to judicial review, nor is it correct in regard to issues about competency to describe judicial review ... as a public law remedy.

The test is however by no means straightforward,[19] but it does at least make it clear that the Court of Session has not become entangled in the public/private distinction which has caused so many difficulties south of the Border. We shall return to the practical effects (if any) of this jurisdictional problem below.

A related point, however, concerns the possibility of transferring cases from one form of procedure to another. In England, this had also caused problems (exacerbated by the way in which the House of Lords had introduced the principle of exclusivity), because the Rules of Court provide that a case begun by judicial review may be transferred to another procedure but that the reverse transfer is not provided for.[20] As a result, cases such as *O'Reilly v Mackman*, which were held to be appropriate for judicial review rather than ordinary civil action, would fall as they would be well outside the time limit for commencing a fresh judicial review application. Indeed, the English courts have indicated that even the permissible transfer out of judicial review should be exercised only sparingly.[21]

---

[18] *Tehrani v Argyll and Clyde Health Board (No 2)* 1990 SLT 118.
[19] See *Naik v University of Stirling* 1994 SLT 449; *Joobeen v University of Stirling* 1994 SLT 120; *Blair v Lochaber District Council* 1995 SLT 407; W Finnie, 'Triangles as Touchstones of Review' 1993 SLT (News) 51; C Himsworth, 'Public Employment, the Supervisory Jurisdiction and Points West' 1992 SLT (News) 257; and C Himsworth, 'Further West? More Geometry of Judicial Review' 1995 SLT (News) 127.
[20] RSC Ord 53, r 9(5).
[21] *R v East Berkshire Health Authority ex parte Walsh* [1985] QB 152 (CA).

True to its spirit of seeking a procedure with the maximum flexibility, the Dunpark Committee recommended that transfer either into or out of judicial review be permitted at the discretion of the judge.[22] This provision did not appear in the final version of the rule, although the lack of a strict time limit and the generally more flexible and speedy approach of the Court of Session should prevent the worst problems which have arisen south of the Border.

The other problem of the scope of the new procedure, that of the recommended incorporation of the statutory procedures for planning and roads, was resolved contrary to the wishes of the Dunpark Committee, and the procedures were not incorporated into the new procedure but must be sought separately. This study will consider later whether there are material differences in the way in which they are handled by the court, and whether it would be advantageous to incorporate them into judicial review; it is clear that the short time limit of six weeks in these cases will remain, and this was in fact agreed by the Dunpark Committee.

Before dealing with the effects of the reform, one further point should be made. Stress has been placed on the importance of the role of the judge as master of procedure in judicial review. The Dunpark Committee recommended (despite opposition from the Faculty of Advocates) that English reform be followed in the appointment by the Lord President of a panel of nominated judges to hear and decide judicial review petitions: 'it is our unanimous opinion that a panel of nominated Judges would enable those judges to develop an expertise in this branch of law and with this procedure which should produce a greater consistency than casual allotment to any available Judge'.[23] This was subject to the exception that if no nominated judge was available during vacation, the vacation judge could order intimation and service and set the wheels in motion for the subsequent hearing of the application, preferably by a nominated judge.[24] The final version of the rule simply provides that petitions shall be heard by a nominated judge or, where such a judge is not available, by any other judge of the court including the vacation judge.[25] English research has established that judges other than those on the nominated list were extensively involved in judicial review decisions, and that cases were unevenly distributed even within the nominated judges.[26] Later in this book we will assess the role of the nominated judges in Scotland.

The new procedure in practice

As mentioned above, the new procedure was implemented from 30 April 1985; almost immediately it was used for a major test case involving ownership of

---
[22] Draft rule 20.
[23] Draft rule 2.
[24] Draft rule 7.
[25] RCS, r 58.5.
[26] *Judicial Review in Perspective*, op. cit., Ch 6.

2 THE KEY CHARACTERISTICS AND RESEARCH ISSUES

assets in the Trustee Savings Banks in the process of privatisation.[27] An academic study of the new procedure was commissioned by the Economic and Social Research Council covering the period April 1985 to April 1987; it came to conclusions suggesting that the procedure had been highly successful in meeting its objectives.[28] Thus, whilst before the introduction of the new procedure only a handful of petitions had been brought in each year, in the eight months from its introduction 27 petitions were raised; this rose to 49 in 1986 and to 88 in 1989. The study found that the aim of producing a speedy procedure had been achieved:

> [t]he single most striking feature of the procedure which emerged from our study is its speed. Of the 77 petitions examined, 63 proceeded to a final interlocutor within the period covered. Of these 16 (25 per cent) were disposed of within four weeks, 31 (49 per cent) within six weeks and 43 (68 per cent) within two months of being raised. Only two were not disposed of within six months of being raised. Insofar as one of the main objectives of reform was to expedite the disposal of applications for judicial review, the evidence of our study suggests that it has been outstandingly successful.[29]

The study considered that the speed of the procedure had not detrimentally affected the quality of decision-making, but noted the low success rate of applications (17%), although a substantial number of other petitions may have resulted in a favourable settlement during the proceedings. The study noted the need for a more systematic and detailed study of the impact of decisions on the administration.

Key questions for research: use of judicial review

This brief account of the development of the judicial review procedure in Scotland suggests a number of fruitful areas for research; others are suggested by the parallel research carried out in England and Wales and in Northern Ireland. We shall now identify key questions for examination, and our findings in relation to them will be presented in the following two chapters which concern the court. Other matters, such as the availability of legal aid, the role of advisers and the impact of decisions, will be dealt with separately later in this book.

The first question is that of the numbers of petitions brought. As we have seen, the earlier Scottish research suggested that there had been a very marked increase in the use of judicial review with the introduction of the new procedure; in England and Wales there had also been a dramatic increase with applications for leave increasing over fourfold between 1981 and 1992, so much

---

[27] *Ross v Lord Advocate* [1986] 1 WLR 1077.
[28] 'Judicial Review in the Court of Session', *op. cit.*
[29] *Ibid.*, p 62.

so that judicial anxiety had been expressed about the resulting overloading and delays.[30] We need to establish whether a sustained increase had occurred in Scotland; if so, it would tend to justify a procedure introduced to make the use of judicial review easier for applicants. Secondly, the subject-matter of the cases needed examination. The English research had established that much of the increase was accounted for by relatively large numbers of applications in particular areas, notably immigration and housing, and that in other areas relatively few applications were made. If this is the case in Scotland, it could provide an explanation for any increase in numbers which is not necessarily compatible with the effective development of judicial review as a *general* remedy against administrative illegality.

The next area for examination is the nature of the petitioners and their advisers. The English research found that the vast majority of applications for judicial review are brought in the name of individuals; judicial review is not widely used by pressure groups to undertake 'test cases' in their own names, something likely to be reinforced in Scotland by the stricter rules on standing. In England, companies do not use the procedure frequently, nor does central government, although in England and Wales local government is a relatively frequent initiator of judicial review, particularly against central government, and mainly in relation to town and country planning issues.[31] Similar findings had been made in the earlier Scottish research. The predominant use of judicial review by individuals might, however, disguise a concentration of use by particular advisers and in particular geographical areas. Thus, the English study found that immigration and homeless persons cases were heavily concentrated in London, whilst others were more widely spread.[32] Use of the procedure in England is heavily concentrated in certain firms of private practitioners: less than 6% of solicitors' offices receiving legal aid payments undertook even one judicial review application in a year, whilst a small number of firms were high users, with 10 or more applications per year. It is also used by law centres, with over half the law centres in the country being involved in at least one judicial review application in any one year.[33] Once more, this information could help to establish whether judicial review is living up to its potential as a general remedy against administrative illegality.

A further important question for assessing whether judicial review in Scotland is living up to its potential is that of the range of respondents against whom petitions are sought. The English research found that it is misleading to view judicial review as primarily a tool for challenging and constraining central government; it is more of an additional constraint on *local* government. Central government cases are highly concentrated in immigration, with relatively limited coverage elsewhere, whereas, even disregarding homelessness cases, the number of applications against local government has increased significantly. Courts

---

[30] *Puhlhofer v London Borough of Hillingdon* [1986] 1 All ER 467.
[31] *Judicial Review in Perspective, op. cit.*, Ch 2.
[32] *Ibid.*, pp 21–23.
[33] *Ibid.*, Ch 3.

and inferior tribunals are also respondents in a substantial number of cases, but other public bodies and non-governmental organisations are rarely faced with the procedure.[34] The earlier Scottish research found that judicial review was used more frequently against local than central government, differences from England and Wales being attributable to the relative lack of immigration cases.

Finally, some assessment will have to be made of the outcomes of judicial review petitions. This is, of course, by no means a straightforward process. Experience from south of the Border is difficult to compare with that in Scotland due to the absence of the leave filter in the latter jurisdiction; the English study found that only a minority of applications reach a full hearing and that decisions at the leave stage and processes of settlement and/or withdrawal either side of leave are far more important in shaping the eventual outcome.[35] The earlier Scottish study, as already mentioned, noted that the low success rate was moderated by settlements in a larger number of cases; these will also have to be examined to determine success rates more accurately.

Key questions for research: the procedure

The matters described above all concern the use made of judicial review. A further set of questions concerns the way in which the procedure introduced in Scotland in 1985 actually operates.

First, does the absence of a formal requirement of leave mean that many weak or unarguable cases survive until dismissal at a hearing on the merits? Is there thus an exceptionally low success rate of cases that reach the hearing? As mentioned above, the earlier Scottish research found a success rate of only 17% at the hearing, but noted that a further 26% of cases resulted in an accommodation between the parties or an undertaking given to the court by the respondent; these cases could not be regarded as totally unsuccessful.[36] Assessing whether the absence of a leave requirement creates difficulties will also involve examination of these cases. We will also need to examine whether interim relief is itself an important objective independent of the final decision reached; if it is, this will provide a further category of success which may be of great practical importance but concealed by final success rates.

An important justification for the new procedure was that of speed. How long does it take for cases to be resolved? This has been a serious problem in England, where the increase in cases brought led to serious delays through clogging the system. Thus, as regards applications first lodged in the first quarter of 1991, three-fifths had not been determined within 360 days and almost half took

---
[34] *Ibid.*, pp 23–30.
[35] *Ibid.*, Ch 4.
[36] 'Judicial Review in the Court of Session', *op. cit.*, p 62.

more than 540 days to reach a full hearing.[37] With the appointment of extra judges in 1992, however, matters improved, and by 1994 the projected waiting time for a case to be heard had been cut from 21.3 months in July 1993 to 12 months in relation to hearings before single judges, and from 10.2 months to 7.3 months in relation to hearings before a Divisional Court.[38] This, however, refers only to the time between the putting down of a case as ready for hearing and the hearing date. The earlier Scottish research had shown much greater speed even than this, and it is to be seen whether this has survived any rise in cases brought. There will also be an opportunity to examine the role of any special expedition of urgent cases.

A related matter is that of interim relief pending the hearing. In England, the Rules of Court make provision for the granting of interim relief and it is often granted in homelessness cases; however, it was thought, at the time of the introduction of the rule, that interim injunctions could not be obtained against the Crown or Crown servants as a matter of constitutional principle, limiting the usefulness of the rule. However, the House of Lords held in the *Factortame* case[39] that interim injunctions are available against ministers of the Crown where European Community rights are involved. It was then held in *Re M*[40] that there is jurisdiction to make coercive orders such as interim injunctions against ministers of the Crown acting in their official capacity, although not against the Crown itself. The latter decision was not followed in Scotland in the (non-judicial review) case of *McDonald v Secretary of State for Scotland*.[41] However, the Rules of Court do make provision for interim orders,[42] and the granting of interim orders other than interdict, notably interim liberation, against central government has been an important function of judicial review in Scotland. This relatively neglected role of judicial review will need further examination.

The use of nominated judges will also be assessed. As mentioned earlier, there has been extensive use in England of judges other than those nominated for judicial review. We will examine whether petitions have been successfully concentrated on the nominated judges in Scotland.

Finally, we will examine some of the currently controversial questions relating to the procedure of judicial review, including title and interest, the types of bodies against which it is competent to seek judicial review, and the availability of damages, to see if we can draw some limited conclusions about the extent to which there are real problems relating to these issues.

This will complete the discussion of the procedure before the Court of Session. Later chapters will go outside the courts by examining legal aid for judicial review and the views and attitudes of legal and lay advisers, both of which will enable us to establish whether filters limiting access to judicial review

---

[37] *Judicial Review in Perspective, op. cit.*, p 59.
[38] Law Commission, *Administrative Law: Judicial Review and Statutory Appeals*, Law Com No 226, 1994, HC 669, paras 2.21–2.22.
[39] *R v Secretary of State for Transport ex parte Factortame Ltd* [1991] 1 AC 603.
[40] [1994] 1 AC 377.
[41] 1994 SLT 692.
[42] RCS, 58(7)(b).

exist outside the judicial process. Finally, we will outline a limited study of the effect of judicial review in homeless cases to assess the degree to which it is a real constraint on administrators and the extent to which decisions of the courts have a practical effect.

It is hoped that the reader will now have a basic understanding of judicial review procedure in Scotland and will be conscious of some of the problems relating to it which can be examined in the research. The first set of issues to be studied concerns the use of judicial review, and the next chapter will examine this, with the procedural issues left until Chapter 4.

Chapter 3

THE USE OF JUDICIAL REVIEW

In this chapter we will analyse the use of judicial review, concentrating on the numbers of cases, subject-matter, types of petitioner and respondent, geographical distribution and outcome. Two aims will underlie our assessment of these characteristics: first, whether the new procedure for judicial review introduced in 1985 has lived up to its objectives of providing a more accessible means of challenging alleged administrative illegality; and, secondly, whether similar tendencies can be found to those detected in England and Wales.[1]

The number of petitions

English experience certainly suggests that reform of judicial review procedure, together with other factors, can produce a large increase in caseload. Thus, between 1981 and 1994 the number of applications for leave increased over sixfold, from 533 to 3208 (although this was not constant, including one year in which applications actually declined, and the number of applications reaching a full hearing increased more slowly).[2] The overall increase also disguised big differences in the use of the procedure in relation to different subjects, with changes in the number of immigration cases having a particularly strong effect on the overall numbers.[3]

In Scotland, statistics were not kept for the use of the supervisory jurisdiction before the 1985 reform, but, according to earlier research, 'before 1985 it was

---

[1] Information on the English research can be found in *Judicial Review in Perspective, op. cit.*; see also M Sunkin, 'What is Happening to Applications for Judicial Review?' (1987) 50 *Modern Law Review*, pp 432–467; M Sunkin, L Bridges and G Mézáros, 'Trends in Judicial Review' [1993] *Public Law*, pp 443–448; A LeSueur and M Sunkin, 'Applications for Judicial Review: The Requirement of Leave' [1992] *Public Law*, pp 102–129.

[2] *Judicial Review in Perspective, op cit.*, pp 1–2; corrected and updated from information provided by the Public Law Project to be incorporated in the second edition of this work.

[3] See also Sunkin, 'What is Happening to Applications for Judicial Review?', *op. cit.*

Table 3.1 Total petitions for judicial review

1988	1989	1990	1991	1992	1993	1988-93
66	86	62	78	117	151	560

The numbers differ slightly from those in our earlier published reports; this is because of the correction of minor classification errors.

uncommon for more than a handful of applications to be raised in any one year'.[4] The same research found that in the eight months of 1985 after the introduction of the new procedure, 27 petitions were raised; in 1986, 49; in 1987, 44; in 1988, 66; and in 1989, 88.[5] This suggested that the new procedure had been successful in providing a more accessible means of challenging alleged administrative illegality.

Our own findings, covering petitions raised in the years 1988–93, are reproduced in Table 1.

What this suggests is a fairly steady use of the procedure at the increased level which had settled after the introduction of the new procedure, with a large increase in 1992 and 1993. This appears impressive, but, before examining subject areas and possible reasons for the recent increase, a note of caution should be entered. The 1993 figure of 151 petitions only represents one petition per 34,000 inhabitants of Scotland, a figure far lower than that for England and Wales where the 1992 figure was one application per 21,000, and Northern Ireland where the *per capita* figure is even higher. The divergence can be partly explained by the especial likelihood of London to give rise to homelessness cases, the role of Heathrow as the main airport of entry in immigration cases, and the importance of prisoner cases in Northern Ireland. Nevertheless, the figure does not suggest that the Scottish courts are being flooded by cases in the way which was sometimes feared recently in England. More recent data supplied by the court shows that in 1994 161 petitions were raised, and in the first nine months of 1995, 147. This confirms the steady rise in the numbers; however, as we shall now establish, much depends also on subject-matter.

The subject-matter of judicial review petitions

The subject-matter of the petitions is set out in Table 2, with further breakdown of housing and licensing cases in Table 3.

The first question is whether there is any explanation suggested here for the large increase in petitions in 1992 and 1993. It is immediately obvious that there were particularly large increases in immigration and homelessness cases in those years, and that this was sufficient to account for most of the increase.

---
[4] 'Judicial Review in the Court of Session', *op. cit.*, p 58.
[5] *Ibid.*

3 THE USE OF JUDICIAL REVIEW

Table 3.2 Subject-matter of petitions

Subject	1988	1989	1990	1991	1992	1993	1988–93
Education	8 / 12.1%	3 / 3.5%	0 / 0.0%	4 / 5.1%	2 / 1.7%	9 / 6.0%	26 / 4.6%
Employment	2 / 3.0%	2 / 2.3%	5 / 8.1%	0 / 0.0%	2 / 1.7%	1 / 0.7%	12 / 2.1%
Housing	8 / 12.1%	10 / 11.6%	9 / 14.5%	10 / 12.8%	26 / 22.2%	26 / 17.2%	89 / 15.9%
Immigration	15 / 22.7%	21 / 24.4%	12 / 19.4%	17 / 21.8%	36 / 30.8%	55 / 36.4%	156 / 27.9%
Legal aid	2 / 3.0%	0 / 0.0%	1 / 1.6%	2 / 2.6%	1 / 0.9%	3 / 2.0%	9 / 1.6%
Licensing	8 / 12.1%	28 / 32.6%	7 / 11.3%	13 / 16.7%	11 / 9.4%	25 / 16.6%	92 / 16.4%
Local government	4 / 6.1%	1 / 1.2%	5 / 8.1%	3 / 3.8%	8 / 6.8%	9 / 6.0%	30 / 5.4%
Planning & land use	8 / 12.1%	7 / 8.1%	10 / 16.1%	8 / 10.3%	8 / 6.8%	5 / 3.3%	46 / 8.2%
Prisoners	1 / 1.5%	0 / 0.0%	3 / 4.8%	2 / 2.6%	0 / 0.0%	1 / 0.7%	7 / 1.3%
Social security	1 / 1.5%	1 / 1.2%	2 / 3.2%	8 / 10.3%	3 / 2.6%	6 / 4.0%	21 / 3.8%
Taxes	0 / 0.0%	1 / 1.2%	0 / 0.0%	2 / 2.6%	0 / 0.0%	1 / 0.7%	4 / 0.7%
Transport	0 / 0.0%	2 / 2.3%	0 / 0.0%	4 / 5.1%	3 / 2.6%	0 / 0.0%	9 / 1.6%
Welfare	4 / 6.1%	3 / 3.5%	3 / 4.8%	2 / 2.6%	4 / 3.4%	2 / 1.3%	18 / 3.2%
Other	5 / 7.6%	7 / 8.1%	5 / 8.1%	3 / 3.8%	13 / 11.1%	8 / 5.3%	41 / 7.3%
Total cases	66 / 99.9%	86 / 100%	62 / 100%	78 / 100.1%	117 / 100%	151 / 100.2%	560 / 100%

The only other areas showing marked increases during those years were education (in 1993 only), liquor licensing (in 1989 and 1993) and local government. The immigration increase is particularly striking; more recent data show that in 1994 immigration petitions dropped to 36; however, our preliminary information is that in the first nine months of 1995 they showed a marked increase to 74 petitions.

At this point it should be stressed that in immigration cases the majority of petitions perform a different function from those in other areas, and, indeed, from immigration petitions in England and Wales. In effect, they are disguised bail applications in which the objective is to secure interim relief, usually in the

Table 3.3 Housing and licensing petitions

Subject	1988	1989	1990	1991	1992	1993	1988–93
Housing	8	10	9	10	26	26	89
Homelessness	5	6	6	9	22	22	70
	62.5%	60.0%	66.7%	90.0%	84.6%	84.6%	78.7%
Other	3	4	3	1	4	4	19
	37.5%	40.0%	33.3%	10.0%	15.4%	15.4%	21.3%
Licensing	8	28	7	13	11	25	92
Liquor	5	19	1	10	5	22	62
	62.5%	67.9%	14.3%	76.9%	45.5%	88.0%	67.4%
Other	3	9	6	3	6	3	30
	37.5%	32.1%	85.7%	23.1%	54.5%	12.0%	32.6%
Total cases	66	86	62	78	117	151	560

form of interim liberation. *Sokha v Secretary of State for the Home Department* gives a good indication of this type of petition. In that case the petitioner had been detained as an illegal entrant and had applied for asylum; he was prepared to live with his uncle who would provide a monetary security, and sought reduction of the decision to detain him, declarator, interim suspension and interim liberation. The petition was not granted on jurisdictional grounds as the English jurisdiction was appropriate in this case, but the judge noted that the case was typical of a number of others in which interim liberation had been granted and that, although there appeared to be no grounds for reduction of the substantive decision, 'this case appears to fall into a category where I would not expect an application to this court for interim liberation to fail ...'.[6] As was made clear in the case, in England such an application could not be made successfully without grounds for review of the substantive decision.[7] According to Lord Prosser, '[w]hile I find that odd, it is not necessarily incomprehensible or unjustifiable. Policy and practice in Scotland as I understand them to be, and as they have been described to the court, may reflect an unease felt by the Scottish courts at the idea that deprivation of liberty, for periods which would not here be regarded as acceptable pending a criminal trial, could be regarded as reasonable in order to exclude a perhaps slight risk of an illegal entrant absconding'.[8]

The proportion of immigration cases became substantial from 1992. Thus, in that year, 28 of the 36 immigration petitions appeared to be applications for interim liberation and, in 1993, 41 out of 55 petitions were such applications. The popularity of this unique type of petition explains much of the increase in that year, and is certainly more important than the legislative change represented by the coming into effect, in July 1993, of the Asylum and Immigration

---

[6] 1992 SLT 1049 at 1050 (*per* Lord Prosser).
[7] See, *e.g.*, *Re Vilvarajah's application for bail* (1987), *The Times*, 31 October.
[8] At 1052.

Appeals Act 1993 which provided a new right of appeal from the Immigration Appeal Tribunal to the Court of Session in asylum and immigration cases, but also abolished appeal rights for visitors, short-term and prospective students and their dependents. The latter abolition of appeal rights occurred too late to explain the increase in immigration cases; however, the new appeal right in other cases may provide part of the explanation for the 1994 drop in petitions. Evidence from interviewees in the study suggests that the 1995 increase is due largely to asylum cases where leave to appeal to the courts has been refused, and suggests that the Home Office has dealt with a backlog of cases through the use of temporary staff with a resulting decline in the quality of decision-making. The general pattern of an overall increase in immigration cases on judical review since 1991 has also been replicated in England.

The rise in housing cases was accounted for by a large increase in petitions concerning homelessness (22 in each of 1992 and 1993); numbers have stayed roughly similar in 1994 and 1995. We will return to the subject in Chapter 6 below, because it is possible that the rise in numbers is attributable to an accumulation of changes in the way local advice networks are functioning.

Looking more generally at subject-matter, we find that the largest categories of petitions are immigration (27.9% over all years, including the interim liberation petitions discussed above), licensing (16.4%) and housing (15.9%). The latter two categories are dominated by liquor licensing and homelessness cases. The concentration appears to be increasing; thus, in 1993 immigration represented 36.4% of petitions, licensing 16.6% and housing showed a slight decline to 17.2%. By contrast, many important areas of public administration showed little use of judicial review; thus, annual numbers never went above single figures in education, local government (excluding housing and planning), prisoners, social security, tax, transport or welfare.

This concentration of cases mirrors the situation south of the Border, where the research noted that, 'applications relating to just three areas – crime, immigration and housing – have dominated the use of judicial review throughout this time [*sc.* 1987–91], accounting together for between 57% and 68% of all leave applications'.[9] Crime did not, however, represent a source of petitions in Scotland; where the supervisory jurisdiction is sought in a criminal matter, application is made to the supervisory jurisdiction of the High Court of Justiciary, which is outside the scope of this study.[10] The large number of licensing cases in Scotland, especially those in liquor licensing, can be explained by gaps in the appeals system against licensing decisions. The most frequent reason for a petition for judicial review is refusal to grant a regular extension of permitted hours for licensed premises. Other reasons for review have included refusal to treat applications to the licensing board as lodged in time, and the granting of gaming licences, against which an objector has no right of appeal.[11] The

---

[9] *Judicial Review in Perspective, op. cit.*, p 5.
[10] *Reynolds v Christie* 1988 SLT 68.
[11] The relevent statutes are the Licensing (Scotland) Act 1976; and the Betting, Gaming and Lotteries Act 1963.

percentage of education cases is small and varies from year to year; it would be tempting to attribute this to the presence of a right of appeal to the sheriff from decisions of appeal committees relating to school admissions, decisions which carry no right of appeal in England.[12] However, although the numbers of education petitions south of the Border are substantially higher, they also form a very small proportion of judicial review applications there and tend to be concentrated on issues relating to educational special needs.[13] The very low numbers of prisoner cases is, perhaps, a surprise; in Northern Ireland these constituted as much as 42.4% of cases for reasons connected with the peculiar problems of the Province;[14] in England and Wales, however, numbers declined sharply from 1987 and constituted a very small number of cases, despite the high profile of some prisoners' cases during the 1970s and 1980s. This decline seems to have been due to the development of more satisfactory internal disciplinary procedures in prisons, in itself influenced by earlier high-profile cases.

It is worth repeating at this point one of the findings of the English research which is relevant to Scotland given the similar concentration of cases:

> The 23 subject areas listed ... are testimony to the potential breadth of judicial review. Yet, this presents one of the main contradictions to be explained about judicial review: given the potential scope of litigation and that the procedure is perceived as being reasonably accessible and the law dynamic, why are there so few challenges in many key areas of governmental activity affecting vital rights and interests of individuals and groups?[15]

Who seeks judicial review?

Table 4 sets out information on the types of petitioner in judicial review cases. It will be seen that the overwhelming majority of petitions are raised by private individuals; there appeared to be no representative actions on behalf of pressure groups and, as mentioned in Chapter 2, the stricter rules on standing in Scotland make it difficult for such groups to bring petitions in their own names.[16] The nearest examples to such cases were two petitions raised by teaching unions or professional organisations on behalf of their members, a petition by NUPE and others relating to local government tendering, and (after the period of our research) the successful petition by Highland Regional Council to prevent the withdrawal of the Fort William rail sleeper service.[17] However, in all these cases members of the petitioning organisation were directly affected by

---
[12] Education (Scotland) Act 1980, s 28F.
[13] *Judicial Review in Perspective, op. cit.*, p 5.
[14] B Hadfield and E Weaver, 'Trends in Judicial Review in Northern Ireland' [1994] *Public Law*, pp 12–16.
[15] *Judicial Review in Perspective, op. cit.*, p 7.
[16] See *Scottish Old People's Welfare Council, Petitioners* 1987 SLT 179; *cf.* in England *R v Secretary of State for Foreign and Commonwealth Affairs ex parte World Development Movement Ltd* [1995] 1 All ER 611.
[17] *Highland Regional Council v British Railways Board* (1995) *The Times*, 6 November.

3 THE USE OF JUDICIAL REVIEW

Table 3.4 Petitioners

For code see note	1	2	3	4	5	6	7	Total
1988	42	18	0	6	0	0	0	66
	63.6%	27.3%	0.0%	9.1%	0.0%	0.0%	0.0%	100%
1989	48	34	1	1	2	0	0	86
	55.8%	39.5%	1.2%	1.2%	2.3%	0.0%	0.0%	100%
1990	37	15	0	6	1	1	2	62
	59.7%	24.2%	0.0%	9.7%	1.6%	1.6%	3.2%	100%
1991	46	28	0	2	1	1	0	78
	59.0%	35.9%	0.0%	2.6%	1.3%	1.3%	0.0%	100.1%
1992	83	28	0	4	1	1	0	117
	70.9%	23.9%	0.0%	3.4%	0.9%	0.9%	0.0%	100%
1993	107	33	0	6	1	4	0	151
	70.9%	21.9%	0.0%	4.0%	0.7%	2.6%	0.0%	100.1%
1988– 1993	363	156	1	25	6	7	2	560
	64.8%	27.9%	0.2%	4.5%	1.1%	1.3%	0.4%	100.2%

Coding: 1 = private individual; 2 = company/commercial; 3 = Government Department; 4 = local authority; 5 = other public sector; 6 = non-governmental organisation; 7 = other.

the decision or it had direct consequences for the local authority area. The increase in immigration and homelessness petitions in the final two years of the study accounts for the larger proportion of individual petitioners during those years.

In England and Wales the proportion of applications made by private individuals was even higher, at between 84% and 88% in the period covered by the research there.[18] By contrast, companies represented less than 10% of English applicants in all the years studied. The much higher Scottish figure is due to the limited role of criminal cases and the larger role played by judicial review of licensing decisions (especially liquor licensing) and planning decisions in Scotland, the particularly high 1989 figure reflecting the unusually large number of liquor licensing cases in that year.[19]

In Scotland, the number of cases brought by Government Departments is small, with only one example during the whole research – a petition brought by the Accountant in Bankruptcy. This can be explained by the lack of any equivalent in Scotland to the Attorney-General as petitioner, a factor of importance in the rest of the United Kingdom and especially Northern Ireland; central government cases involving UK-wide issues are, in any case, likely to be brought in London. The proportion of applications by central government in England and Wales was also very low, however, at just over 1%.[20]

---

[18] *Judicial Review in Perspective, op. cit.*, p 18.
[19] The category 'Company/commercial' includes all commercially motivated petitioners, including unincorporated sole traders petitioning in their own names or under their trading names.
[20] *Judicial Review in Perspective, op. cit.*, p 19.

The third largest category of petitioners in Scotland was that of the local authorities, although these cases represented only 4.5% of our total. In England and Wales the number of applications by local authorities varied widely from year to year, but the numbers were much greater (for example, 55 cases in 1989 and a projected figure of 76 for 1991).[21] Most of these concerned town and country planning issues, although education cases rose sharply towards the end of the English study. In Scotland, the largest number of such cases involved planning matters, with others covering a wide range of subjects including tendering, taxi licensing and teachers' pay and conditions. Other types of petitioner were of minimal importance; the increase in cases to four in 1993 brought by non-governmental organisations is explained by three cases concerned with local taxation brought by miners' welfare societies.

The research confirms that judicial review is a remedy used mainly by individual petitioners, with a very limited role for other types of petitioner. Although in some types of application companies were a larger proportion of users than is the case south of the Border, this was due to particular deficiencies in statutory appeal rights. The next question is the degree to which the origins of the petitions are concentrated geographically. It will be recalled that the English research had established a strong degree of concentration in London, partially explicable by homelessness and immigration cases being particularly likely to arise in the metropolis, but also reflecting a very large degree of concentration of judicial review work in a few solicitors. The origins of the Scottish cases are shown in Table 5, broken down by district council area; the authority is that of the residence of the petitioner, although if the petitioner was in prison, the authority of the prison (if known) was used.

At first sight this suggests a very wide geographical spread of cases; no less than 45 district council areas have been the origin of at least one judicial review petition in the six years studied. On closer examination, however, the vast majority of district council areas gave rise to small numbers of petitions, whilst Glasgow and Edinburgh were overrepresented with 28.4% (13.3% of population), and 10.7% (8.2% of population), respectively. A somewhat surprising finding is the relatively small proportion of cases from the other large Scottish cities; 2.9% (a total of 16 cases over six years) from Aberdeen (4.2% of population), and 2.7% (15 cases) from Dundee (3.4% of population). A significant number of petitions originated from outside Scotland, or, indeed, outside Britain. The latter were, of course, immigration cases where entry had not been permitted; the former included, for example, challenge of local government tendering decisions by an English-based company and challenge to civil aviation policies in Scotland by a Sussex-based airline. In the latter example, the petitioners had, in fact, been advised that they were out of time in England before bringing the petition in Scotland, but, given the fact that the issues had a strong connection with Scotland, there was no problem in proceeding in the Court of Session.[22]

---
[21] *Ibid.*, pp 20–21.
[22] *Air 2000 v Secretary of State for Transport* 1989 SLT 698, 1990 SLT 335. The authors are grateful to the Lord President for supplying further information relating to this case.

3 THE USE OF JUDICIAL REVIEW

Table 3.5 Geographical origin of petitions

District Council	1988	1989	1990	1991	1992	1993	1988–1993
Aberdeen	3	2	4	1	4	2	16
	4.5%	2.3%	6.5%	1.3%	3.4%	1.3%	2.9%
Angus	0	0	1	0	1	0	2
	0%	0%	1.6%	0%	0.9%	0%	0.4%
Argyll & Bute	1	0	0	1	0	0	2
	1.5%	0%	0%	1.3%	0%	0%	0.4%
Banff & Buchan	2	0	2	3	0	1	8
	3.0%	0%	3.2%	3.8%	0%	0.7%	1.4%
Caithness	1	1	1	0	1	0	4
	1.5%	1.2%	1.6%	0%	0.9%	0%	0.7%
Clackmannan	0	1	0	0	0	1	2
	0%	1.2%	0%	0%	0%	0.7%	0.4%
Clydebank	0	0	0	0	0	4	4
	0%	0%	0%	0%	0%	2.6%	0.7%
Clydesdale	0	0	0	2	1	3	6
	0%	0%	0%	2.6%	0.9%	2.0%	1.1%
Cumbernauld	0	2	1	1	0	0	4
	0%	2.3%	1.6%	1.3%	0%	0%	0.7%
Cumnock & Doon Valley	1	0	0	1	0	0	2
	1.5%	0%	0%	1.3%	0%	0%	0.4%
Cunninghame	0	2	0	3	2	2	9
	0%	2.3%	0%	3.8%	1.7%	1.3%	1.6%
Dumbarton	0	1	0	0	0	2	3
	0%	1.2%	0%	0%	0%	1.3%	0.5%
Dundee	0	1	1	7	2	4	15
	0%	1.2%	1.6%	9.0%	1.7%	2.6%	2.7%
Dunfermline	1	1	0	1	3	1	7
	1.5%	1.2%	0%	1.3%	2.6%	0.7%	1.3%
East Kilbride	0	0	0	1	0	3	4
	0%	0%	0%	1.3%	0%	2.0%	0.7%
Eastwood	0	0	0	0	1	0	1
	0%	0%	0%	0%	0.9%	0%	0.2%
Edinburgh	10	8	11	11	10	10	60
	15.2%	9.3%	17.7%	14.1%	7.7%	6.6%	10.7%
Ettrick & Lauderdale	0	1	0	0	0	1	2
	0%	1.2%	0%	0%	0%	0.7%	0.4%
Falkirk	1	2	0	0	1	3	7
	1.5%	2.3%	0%	0%	0.9%	2.0%	1.3%
Glasgow	30	28	13	16	29	43	159
	45.5%	32.6%	21.0%	20.5%	24.8%	28.5%	28.4%

Table 3.5 Continued

District Council	1988	1989	1990	1991	1992	1993	1988–1993
Hamilton	1 1.5%	0 0%	3 4.8%	5 6.4%	1 0.9%	1 0.7%	11 2.0%
Inverclyde	0 0%	1 1.2%	2 3.2%	5 6.4%	20 17.1%	23 15.2%	51 9.1%
Inverness	0 0%	0 0%	3 4.8%	0 0%	2 1.7%	1 0.7%	6 1.1%
Kilmarnock & Loudoun	1 1.5%	0 0%	0 0%	1 1.3%	1 0.9%	0 0%	3 0.5%
Kincardine & Deeside	0 0%	1 1.2%	1 1.6%	0 0%	2 1.7%	1 0.7%	5 0.8%
Kirkcaldy	1 1.5%	1 1.2%	0 0%	0 0%	1 0.9%	2 1.3%	5 0.9%
Kyle & Carrick	0 0%	0 0%	2 3.2%	1 1.3%	6 5.1%	6 4.0%	15 2.7%
Lochaber	0 0%	0 0%	1 1.6%	0 0%	2 1.7%	1 0.7%	4 0.7%
Midlothian	0 0%	1 1.2%	1 1.6%	0 0%	0 0%	1 0.7%	3 0.5%
Monklands	1 1.5%	4 4.7%	0 0%	2 2.6%	2 1.7%	2 1.3%	11 2.0%
Moray	0 0%	0 0%	2 3.2%	0 0%	0 0%	0 0%	2 0.4%
Motherwell	3 4.5%	0 0%	0 0%	1 1.3%	5 4.3%	5 2.6%	14 2.5%
Nithsdale	0 0%	2 2.3%	3 4.8%	3 3.8%	1 0.9%	5 2.6%	14 2.5%
North East Fife	0 0%	3 3.5%	0 0%	0 0%	1 0.9%	0 0%	4 0.7%
Perth & Kinross	0 0%	1 1.2%	2 3.2%	0 0%	1 0.9%	4 2.6%	8 1.4%
Renfrew	2 3.0%	1 1.2%	0 0%	0 0%	1 0.9%	4 2.6%	8 1.4%
Ross & Cromarty	0 0%	9 10.5%	0 0%	1 1.3%	0 0%	0 0%	10 1.8%
Roxburgh	0 0%	0 0%	0 0%	0 0%	1 0.9%	0 0%	1 0.2%
Stirling	1 1.5%	1 1.2%	2 3.2%	2 2.6%	0 0%	0 0%	6 1.1%
Strathkelvin	0 0%	1 1.2%	0 0%	1 1.3%	0 0%	0 0%	2 0.4%

3 THE USE OF JUDICIAL REVIEW

Table 3.5 Continued

District Council	1988	1989	1990	1991	1992	1993	1988–1993
Sutherland	0 0%	0 0%	1 1.6%	0 0%	0 0%	0 0%	1 0.2%
Tweedale	0 0%	0 0%	0 0%	1 1.3%	0 0%	0 0%	1 0.2%
West Lothian	2 3.0%	2 2.3%	0 0%	0 0%	3 2.6%	2 1.3%	9 1.6%
Western Isles	4 6.1%	1 1.2%	0 0%	1 1.3%	0 0%	1 0.7%	7 1.3%
Wigtown	0 0%	0 0%	0 0%	2 2.6%	2 1.7%	2 1.3%	6 1.1%
England & Wales	0 0%	6 7.0%	4 6.5%	3 3.8%	5 4.3%	4 2.6%	22 3.9%
World	0 0%	1 1.2%	1 1.6%	1 1.3%	5 4.3%	6 4.0%	14 2.5%
Total	66 99.8%	86 99.4%	62 99.7%	78 100.2%	117 99.8%	151 99.3%	560 100.4%

Against whom is judicial review sought?

Analysis was also undertaken of the respondents to all judicial review petitions, and the results are set out in Table 6.

It will be seen that the largest category by a considerable margin was that of local authorities, and this remained constant in the mid-forties percentage during the six years of the study. It is noticeable that this percentage is considerably higher than the overall proportion of petitions concerning housing matters in Table 2 (15.9%). Petitions are raised against local authorities on a wide range of matters such as education, licensing and planning. In this sense the procedure has characteristics of an all-purpose remedy *in relation to local authorities*. In the English study, the proportion of local authority respondents was smaller, ranging in the period studied from 19.5% in 1987 to 35.1% in the first quarter of 1991; although homelessness cases predominated, there was also a wide spread of different subject areas, with education showing a marked increase in cases in 1989 and 1991.[23] The lower proportion of local authority respondents in England is partly a reflection of the more limited role of licensing applications in judicial review there, but one must also consider the role of challenges against central government. In Scotland, the overall proportion of challenges to central government was 36.4%. This showed a marked increase from 30.8% to 40.4% from 1991 to 1993, reflecting the increase in immigration

---
[23] *Judicial Review in Perspective, op. cit.*, pp 26–27.

Table 3.6 Respondents

For code see note	1	2	3	4	5	6	7	Total
1988	31	24	3	6	2	0	0	66
	47.0%	36.4%	4.5%	9.1%	3.0%	0.0%	0.0%	100%
1989	42	30	7	4	3	0	0	86
	48.8%	34.9%	8.1%	4.7%	3.5%	0.0%	0.0%	100%
1990	25	24	8	4	0	0	1	62
	40.3%	38.7%	12.9%	6.5%	0.0%	0.0%	1.6%	100%
1991	37	24	10	6	0	0	1	78
	47.4%	30.8%	12.8%	7.7%	0.0%	0.0%	1.3%	100%
1992	51	41	12	8	2	1	2	117
	43.6%	35.0%	10.3%	6.8%	1.7%	0.9%	1.7%	100%
1993	66	61	5	9	2	0	8	151
	43.7%	40.4%	3.3%	6.0%	1.3%	0.0%	5.3%	100%
1988– 1993	252	204	45	37	9	1	12	560
	45.0%	36.4%	8.0%	6.6%	1.6%	0.2%	2.1%	100%

Explanation of coding: 1 = local authority; 2 = Government Department; 3 = inferior tribunal/court; 4 = other public sector; 5 = non-governmental organisation; 6 = other; 7 = Government Department and tribunal.

cases in that period. In England and Wales the proportion of applications against central government ranged from 45.4% in 1987 to 26.7% in the first quarter of 1991, the former being due to an especially large number of immigration cases; these also predominated in other years. When immigration cases are omitted, applications against central government departments in England ranged from 12% to 8% in each year; in Scotland, 19% to 4%.

As a result of these findings, the English study stated that, 'it is misleading to view judicial review as being primarily a tool for challenging and constraining central government. ... In this respect, it may be argued that the constitutional significance of judicial review in this period has been less as a check on the use of executive power by central government than as an additional constraint on local government'.[24] Our findings would seem to echo this by showing not only that judicial review is sought more often against local authorities than against central government, but that it is sought in relation to a range of their functions rather than only in housing matters. More than three-quarters of the petitions against central government concerned immigration, and a large proportion of these were disguised bail applications. It is interesting that the concentration of central government cases on immigration is also reflected in England, thus suggesting that the limited range of central government functions subject to challenge is not due to the centralisation of some government departments in London without Edinburgh equivalents.

---

[24] *Ibid.*, p 30.

3 THE USE OF JUDICIAL REVIEW

The next largest category of respondents was that of inferior courts and tribunals, with 8% overall, but showing dramatic variations from year to year. This final point is related to the extremely variegated nature of the respondents in this category, which also suggests that no single factor accounts for the increase in 1989–90 and the fall in 1992–93. Examples of respondents falling within this category include Sheriff Courts, the Immigration Appeal Tribunal, and housing benefit review boards.[25] In England and Wales the proportions were much higher, with 28%–36% in the years studied, although the criminal courts counted for 12%–15% of applications; as has already been stated, judicial review does not play an equivalent role in criminal matters in Scotland. Licensing bodies were included in this category in England whilst in Scotland they fall within the category of local authority.

The remaining types of respondent are other public sector and non-governmental organisations; the former included health boards and the Scottish Legal Aid Board, whilst the latter are a varied assortment, including Edinburgh Airport Ltd and arbiters. These were respondents in very few cases, with no signs of an increase in challenges to less 'public' bodies after the decision in *West v Secretary of State for Scotland* 1992 SLT 636. The final category represents those cases where there was a petition sought against both a government department and an inferior tribunal; these were immigration cases where both the Immigration Appeal Tribunal and the Home Secretary were respondents.

Outcomes

The next subject for analysis in this chapter will be the outcomes of judicial review petitions. It will be recalled that in England the leave filter played a fundamental role in determining outcomes; only a minority of cases reached a full hearing and leave and decisions on settlement and withdrawal taken after leave was granted were far more important than the result of the substantive hearing. In Scotland, there is, of course, no equivalent of the leave filter. In the earlier Scottish study a relatively low success rate at the hearing had been found (17% over the whole study) although in a further 26% some sort of accommodation was reached between the parties, or an undertaking was given by the respondent to the court on the basis of which the petition could be concluded; they could not, therefore, be regarded as totally unsuccessful.[26] The question of outcomes is thus likely to be of considerable complexity.

Table 7 gives an overall view of the outcome of petitions.

At first sight, the success rate appears to continue to be low; thus, overall, 12% of petitions were granted in full. Strikingly, this represents a large drop from 1989 (22.1%) and 1990 (19.4%) to 1993 (6.7%). For a fuller understanding of

---

[25] Immigration cases which did not pass to the tribunal from the adjudicator are treated as central government cases as the Secretary of State is the respondent.
[26] 'Judicial Review in the Court of Session', *op. cit.*, p 62. It is likely that petitions granted in part were included amongst the successes in this study.

Table 3.7 Outcomes of petitions

For codes see note	1	2	3	4	5	6	Total
1988	8 12.1%	5 7.6%	35 53.0%	7 10.6%	1 1.5%	10 15.2%	66 100.0%
1989	19 22.1%	4 4.7%	43 50.0%	2 2.3%	6 7.0%	12 14.0%	86 100.1%
1990	12 19.4%	6 9.7%	28 45.2%	9 14.5%	2 3.2%	5 8.1%	62 100.1%
1991	9 11.5%	9 11.5%	39 50.0%	10 12.8%	3 3.8%	8 10.3%	78 99.9%
1992	9 7.7%	9 7.7%	55 47.0%	15 12.8%	12 10.3%	17 14.5	117 100%
1993	10 6.7%	8 5.3%	90 60%	8 5.3%	13 8.7%	21 14%	150* 100%
1988–93	67 12.0%	41 7.3%	290 51.9%	51 9.1%	37 6.6%	73 13.1%	559* 100.0%

* Excludes one case still live at the completion of the study.
Explanation of coding: 1 = petition granted in full; 2 = petition granted in part; 3 = petition not granted; 4 = settlement extra-judicially; 5 = looks like settlement; 6 = taken out of court.

This table refers to outcome of petitions. Columns 1 and 2 can be added together for a successful outcome. Categories 4 and 5 refer to extra-judicial and likely settlements, and so can also be added for positive outcome.

success rates, however, the cases in which the petition was granted in part must be added in, as this often represented a substantial success for the petitioner. For example, in a housing case the petitioner might seek reduction of the local authority's decision and an order that accommodation be provided; the court might, however, issue reduction only to pave the way for a fresh lawful decision, which might go in the petitioner's favour. This produces an overall success rate for the study period of 19.3%. Considerable annual variations remain; adding the two types of success together for 1990, for example, we find a proportion of 29.1%, whilst for 1992 this declines to 15.4% and for 1993 12%.

Before seeking explanations for this in the subject-matter of petitions, it will be useful to take into account other outcomes. These have had to involve a degree of speculation because the case papers do not always make the outcome clear, but it has been possible to categorise them with a considerable degree of confidence. Column 3 of Table 7 represents those cases where it is clear from the papers that the petition was not successful. The percentages are relatively low, with an overall figure of 51.9%, and are more consistent than the success rates would suggest, apart from an increase to 60% in 1993. Column 4 applies to cases where the case papers show that there has been an extra-judicial settlement and it is reasonably clear that the petitioner gained something as a result

3 THE USE OF JUDICIAL REVIEW

Table 3.8 Outcomes excluding cases taken out of court

For code see note	1	2	3	4	5	Total	Total %
1988	8 14.30%	5 8.90%	35 62.50%	7 12.50%	1 1.8%	56 100.00%	84.8%
1989	19 25.70%	4 5.40%	43 58.10%	2 2.70%	6 8.10%	74 100.00%	86.00%
1990	12 21.10%	6 10.50%	28 49.10%	9 15.80%	2 3.50%	57 100.00%	91.90%
1991	9 12.9%	9 12.9%	39 55.7%	10 14.3%	3 4.3%	70 100.1%	89.70%
1992	9 9.0%	9 9.0%	55 55.0%	15 15.0%	12 12.0%	100 100.0%	85.50%
1993	10 7.8%	8 6.2%	90 69.8%	8 6.2%	13 10.1%	129* 100.1%	86.00%
1988–93	67 13.8%	41 8.4%	290 59.7%	51 10.5%	37 7.6%	486* 100%	86.9%

* Excludes one case still live at the completion of the study.
Explanation of coding: 1 = petition granted in full; 2 = petition granted in part; 3 = petition not granted; 4 = settlement extra-judicially; 5 = looks like settlement.
This table refers to outcome of petitions where category 9 has been taken out of the totals and percentages calculated with the total minus category 9 figures. Columns 1 and 2 can be added together for a successful outcome. Categories 4 and 5 refer to extra-judicial and likely settlements, and so could also be added for positive outcome.

of the petition. Once more, there are considerable year-to-year variations, with a peak in 1990 of 14.5% and a decline in 1993 to 5.3%. Column 5 represents those cases where there is some evidence to suggest that there has been a settlement out of court with some benefit to the petitioner, for example through the petition being dismissed by consent with an award of expenses to the petitioner. Again, this category shows considerable year-to-year variation, but without the same pattern of annual variation. Column 6 represents cases taken out of court with no indication of outcome and which follow a reasonably consistent annual pattern; they cover a range of subject-matter, the largest categories being immigration, licensing and planning.

In view of the lack of information on this last category of cases, which may include petitions rendered unnecessary by other decisions or cases where the main object was to obtain interim relief, it is appropriate to disregard them in assessing success rates. Table 8 presents outcomes with such cases disregarded.

The first question which can be answered by these figures is whether there is an extremely low success rate for judicial review petitions which would suggest that the procedure is being used for large numbers of hopeless or speculative cases. The data suggest strongly that this is not the case. Thus, even without counting settlements as successes and taking only cases where the petition was granted in part or in full, we have an overall success rate of 22.2%. In some years this has been considerably higher, with success rates of over 30% in 1989 and 1990. This compares with English figures suggesting that only around 30% of cases reach a substantive hearing, with the rest refused leave or withdrawn before doing so. At the substantive hearing success rates were of 47%–54%, and the overall proportion of applications resulting in rulings against the bodies being challenged ranged from 4.7%–16.3% in the years studied.[27] One also needs to add in, however, those Scottish cases in which there was evidence of settlement producing some benefit to the petitioner. When these are added the 'success rate' becomes 40.3%, with a highest annual 'success rate' of 50.9% in 1990.

This suggests strongly that judicial review is not widely used as a means of bringing hopeless or speculative challenges to public authorities; a leave procedure to filter out such cases is not, it appears, necessary in Scotland. However, at first sight there appears to be a recent tendency for success rates on any measurement to decline. Thus, in 1993 the overall 'success rate', including settlements and excluding cases taken out of court, was only 30.3%. It will be recalled that there was a large increase in the number of immigration cases brought in 1992 and especially in 1993, and so this might provide a key to the changes in the outcomes since we have seen that in a large proportion of such cases the objective was an interim rather than a final order. It is thus necessary to analyse outcomes by subject, which will both provide possible reasons for changing outcomes overall and provide more detailed information on the sorts of cases which are successful. Table 9 presents outcomes by subject, excluding cases taken out of court.

Looking first at overall outcomes for the period of the study, it is noticeable that immigration cases appear to have less successful outcomes than other cases. This is particularly striking in the years 1988–89 and 1992–93, with over three-quarters of petitions in those years not being granted. However, even this is misleading as an indication of success rates, because a different concept of success is applied in those immigration cases where the aim is to gain interim relief, usually in the form of interim liberation. The issue of interim relief will be fully analysed in Chapter 4, but information can usefully be included here about the outcome of applications in immigration cases; this is included in Table 10.

It will be seen here that interim relief, usually in the form of interim liberation, was requested in the vast majority of immigration cases (82.7% overall). The success rate was extremely high, running at 76% of cases in which interim relief was requested; even in 1993, the year of the largest number of immigration petitions, the success rate was 69.6%. Now the figures included in the earlier table for success rates refer only to the **final** outcome of petitions, thus excluding interim relief. Yet, in practice, the most important outcome of many immigration cases will be to obtain interim relief, and this must be taken into account in judging success. When one does so, there is no indication that the

---

[27] *Judicial Review in Perspective, op. cit.*, pp 54, 56; 'Trends in Judicial Review', *op. cit.*, p 445, and data supplied by the Public Law Project.

Table 3.9 1988: Outcomes by subject (excluding cases taken out of court)

Subject	1	2	3	4	5	Total number
Housing	1 14.30%	0 0.00%	4 57.10%	2 28.60%	0 0.00%	7 100.00%
Immigration	0 0%	2 16.7%	10 83.3%	0 0	0 0	12 100%
Licensing	2 28.6%	0 0%	4 57.1%	0 0%	1 14.3%	7 100%
Planning & land use	2 33.3%	1 16.7%	2 33.3%	1 16.7%	0 0%	6 100%
All other subjects	3 12.5%	2 8.3%	15 62.5%	4 16.7%	0 0%	24 100%
Total	8 14.3%	5 8.9%	35 62.5%	7 12.5%	1 1.8%	56 100%

1989: Outcomes by subject (excluding cases taken out of court)

Subject	1	2	3	4	5	Total number
Housing	1 11.10%	1 11.10%	4 44.40%	2 22.20%	1 11.10%	9 99.90%
Immigration	2 10.50%	0 0.00%	15 78.90%	0 0.00%	2 10.50%	19 99.90%
Licensing	8 36.40%	3 13.60%	9 40.90%	0 0.00%	2 9.10%	22 100.00%
Planning & land use	0 0.00%	0 0.00%	6 100.00%	0 0.00%	0 0.00%	6 100.00%
All other subjects	8 44.40%	0 0.00%	9 50.00%	0 0.00%	1 5.60%	18 100.00%
Total	19 25.70%	4 5.40%	43 58.10%	2 2.70%	6 8.10%	74 100.00%

1990: Outcomes by subject (excluding cases taken out of court)

Subject	1	2	3	4	5	Total number
Housing	2 22.2%	0 0%	3 33.3%	4 44.4%	0 0%	9 99.9%
Immigration	2 16.7%	3 25%	4 33.3%	1 8.3%	2 16.7%	12 100%
Licensing	2 33.30%	1 16.70%	2 33.30%	1 16.70%	0 0.00%	6 100%
Planning & land use	1 11.10%	1 11.10%	6 66.70%	1 11.10%	0 0.00%	9 100%

Table 3.9 1990: Outcomes by subject (excluding cases taken out of court) (*continued*)

Subject	1	2	3	4	5	Total number
All other subjects	5 23.80%	1 4.80%	13 61.90%	2 9.50%	0 0.00%	21 100.00%
Total	12 21.10%	6 10.50%	28 49.10%	9 15.8%	2 3.5%	57 100.00%

1991: Outcomes by subject (excluding cases taken out of court)

Subject	1	2	3	4	5	Total number
Housing	2 22.20%	3 33.30%	3 33.30%	1 11.10%	0 0.00%	9 99.90%
Immigration	1 6.70%	2 13.30%	9 60.00%	2 13.30%	1 6.70%	15 100.00%
Licensing	0 0.00%	2 16.70%	8 66.70%	2 16.70%	0 0.00%	12 100.00%
Planning & land use	1 14.30%	0 0.00%	6 85.70%	0 0.00%	0 0.00%	7 100.00%
All other subjects	5 18.50%	2 7.40%	13 48.10%	5 18.50%	2 7.40%	27 99.90%
Total	9 12.90%	9 12.90%	39 55.70%	10 14.30%	3 4.30%	70 100.10%

1992: Outcomes by subject (excluding cases taken out of court)

Subject	1	2	3	4	5	Total number
Housing	2 8.00%	2 8.00%	9 36.00%	9 36.00%	3 12.00%	25 100.00%
Immigration	1 3.00%	1 3.00%	26 78.80%	2 6.10%	3 9.10%	33 100.00%
Licensing	1 11.10%	1 11.10%	4 44.40%	1 11.10%	2 22.20%	9 99.90%
Planning & land use	1 20.00%	1 20.00%	3 60.00%	0 0.00%	0 0.00%	5 100.00%
All other subjects	4 14.30%	4 14.30%	13 46.40%	3 10.70%	4 14.30%	28 100.00%
Total	9 9.00%	9 9.00%	55 55.00%	15 15.00%	12 12.00%	100 100.00%

3 THE USE OF JUDICIAL REVIEW

Table 3.9 1993: Outcomes by subject (excluding cases taken out of court)

Subject	1	2	3	4	5	Total number
Housing	1 4.30%	4 17.40%	12 52.20%	2 8.70%	4 17.40%	23 100.00%
Immigration	2 4.20%	1 2.10%	37 77.10%	4 8.30%	4 8.30%	48 100.00%
Licensing	1 4.50%	0 0.00%	20 90.90%	1 4.50%	0 0.00%	22 99.90%
Planning & land use	1 25.00%	0 0.00%	2 50.00%	0 0.00%	1 25.00%	4 100.00%
All other subjects	5 15.60%	3 9.40%	19 59.40%	1 3.10%	4 12.50%	32* 100.00%
Total	10 7.80%	8 6.20%	90 69.80%	8 6.20%	13 10.10%	129* 100.10%

* Excludes one case still live at the completion of the study.

1988-93: Outcomes by subject (excluding cases taken out of court)

Subject	1	2	3	4	5	Total number
Housing	9 11.0%	10 12.2%	35 42.7%	20 24.4%	8 9.8%	82 100.1%
Immigration	8 5.8%	9 6.5%	101 72.7%	9 6.5%	12 8.6%	139 100.1%
Licensing	14 17.9%	7 9.0%	47 60.3%	5 6.4%	5 6.4%	78 100%
Planning & land use	6 16.2%	3 8.1%	25 67.6%	2 5.4%	1 2.7%	37 100%
All other subjects	30 20%	12 8.0%	82 54.7%	15 10.0%	11 7.3%	150* 100%
Total	67 13.8%	41 8.4%	290 59.7%	51 10.5%	37 7.6%	486* 100%

system is being flooded by large numbers of unarguable immigration petitions, even with the large increase in such petitions from 1992.

Returning to Table 9, none of the subject areas have success rates so low as to suggest that large numbers of unarguable petitions are being raised. It will be recalled that, apart from immigration, the largest categories of petitions by subject were in the areas of licensing and housing (especially homelessness). In the case of licensing, an apparently high rate of petitions dismissed can be explained by the distortion caused by a number of cases in 1993 being brought on the same issue and being unsuccessful; housing success rates are reasonably high, especially taking into account settlements. Indeed, it is striking that there

Table 3.10 Immigration cases and interim relief

Year	No of cases	Interim relief requested	Interim relief granted	Liberation requested	Liberation granted
1988	15	13 (86.7%)	10 (76.9%)	10 (76.9%)	9 (90.0%)
1989	21	19 (90.5%)	17 (89.5%)	16 (84.2%)	15 (93.4%)
1990	12	8 (66.7%)	7 (87.5%)	4 (50%)	4 (100%)
1991	17	13 (76.5%)	11 (84.6%)	7 (53.8%)	7 (100%)
1992	36	30 (83.3%)	21 (70.0%)	28 (93.3%)	17 (60.7%)
1993	55	46 (83.6%)	32 (69.6%)	41 (89.1%)	29 (70.7%)
1988–1993	156	129 (82.7%)	98 (76.0%)	106 (82.2%)	81 (76.4%)

Column 3 percentage calculated by dividing by column 2.
Column 4 percentage calculated by dividing by column 3.
Column 5 percentage calculated by dividing by column 3.
Column 6 percentage calculated by dividing by column 5.

is clear evidence of a particularly high settlement rate in housing cases; clear settlements occurred in 24.4% of cases overall, with a particularly high figure of 44.4% in 1990 (although on a very small number of cases in that year). In English homelessness cases a very high rate of withdrawal following the grant of leave was observed, suggesting a high rate of settlement also at this stage. Indeed, after 1987 more homelessness applications were withdrawn than resulted in a full hearing.[28] The same phenomenon appears to be occurring in Scotland, the significance of which will be examined in Chapter 7, covering the impact study in homelessness cases.

Statutory review

It will be recalled that the Dunpark Report had recommended that statutory review under the Acquisition of Land (Authorisation Procedure) (Scotland) Act 1947 (validity of compulsory purchase orders), the Special Roads Act 1949 (now the Roads (Scotland) Act 1984 (validity of orders)) and the Town and Country Planning (Scotland) Act 1972 (validity of structure plans and other orders) be brought within the new procedure, but with the retention of the

---
[28] *Judicial Review in Perspective, op. cit.*, p 52.

Table 3.11 Statutory applications by subject matter and outcome

Subject matter	1	2	3	4	Total
Town and Country Planning Act	12 (38.7%)	16 (51.6%)	1 (3.2%)	2 (6.5%)	31 (100%)
Compulsory purchase order	0 (0%)	2 (66.7%)	0 (0%)	1 (33.3%)	3 (100%)
Roads*	0 (0%)	0 (0%)	1 (100%)	0 (0%)	1 (100%)
Total number of applications	12 (34.3%)	18 (51.4%)	2 (5.7%)	3 (8.6%)	35 (100%)

*Road Traffic Regulation Act 1984, Sched 9, Part VI, paras 35,36.
Coding: 1 = successful; 2 = dismissed; 3 = extra-judicial settlement; 4 = taken out of court.

special statutory time limit of six weeks. This was not, in fact, implemented and the procedure for such statutory review remains distinct from that of the ordinary petition. In addition to the procedures considered by the Committee, a similar one exists by virtue of the Road Traffic Regulation Act 1984, Schedule 9. At this point it will be useful to provide a little information about the use of these procedures.

The number of such statutory applications was relatively small; we were not able to ascertain the exact number or locate all the case papers. However, we did trace 49 such cases in the period studied, and examined in detail 35 applications, mainly relating to the period 1991–93. We are satisfied that these represented the bulk of the applications submitted under the Acts in the two-year period studied. The subject-matter and outcomes are set out in Table 11.

What is, of course, striking is the dominance of applications under the Town and Country Plannning (Scotland) Act 1972, representing 31 out of 35 applications. In other respects the applications show few differences from petitions for judicial review proper. There is a greater proportion of commercial applicants (43%) and local authority applicants (31%) (unsurprising in view of the issues raised). Interim relief in the form of interim suspension was granted in two applications. The length of the proceedings varied greatly, with four applications determined within 50 days and six more within 100 days; others, however, remained on the books for a considerable period of time.

Are there any good reasons for maintaining the procedure for these applications as one separate from judicial review, rather than implementing the Dunpark recommendations? The number of cases involved is not such as to swamp the judicial review procedure and, of course, bringing them within the judicial review procedure would not actually increase the workload of the court but would merely redistribute it. Indeed, given that the majority of such cases go directly to the Inner House of three judges, incorporating the procedure within judicial review would economise on judicial resources. The grounds for assessing the legality of governmental action in these cases do not differ markedly from those in judicial review cases.[29] The only other reasons apparent to the researchers for retaining the special procedure are that the Inner House is in some way better qualified to deal with these cases than others, and that proceeding directly to the Inner House prevents an unnecessary two-stage procedure should appeal otherwise be likely in these cases. The relatively prosperous and well-advised petitioners characteristic of these cases perhaps makes appeal more likely. As the Dunpark Report noted, however, the argument that the Inner House is better-placed to deal with such cases if valid could also be applied to other cases under the supervisory jurisdiction, and in England such cases are dealt with by a single judge at first instance with no apparent problems. We thus recommend that the statutory applications be brought within the judicial review procedure, but with the six-week time limit retained for them. This should not require legislation, but merely changes in rules of court as, for example, the Town and Country Planning (Scotland) Act 1972 does not specify that applications are to go to the Inner House but states merely that an application is to be made to the Court of Session.[30]

Conclusions

More general policy conclusions will be brought together in the final chapter of this book, but some preliminary points can be made now. The first is that the Scottish procedure, despite the absence of a leave requirement, has not resulted in the courts being swamped by a mass of unarguable cases. The fears expressed by English judges that this was occurring south of the Border referred to problems of caseload management which are not replicated in Scotland. The one apparent exception to this is the recent rise in immigration cases, but in such cases the objective is frequently interim liberation rather than a final order, where the success rate is very high. Outside the subject areas of immigration, licensing and housing (especially homelessness) the problem appears to be one of underuse rather than overuse of judicial review; can it really be the case that in education there were only grounds for two petitions in 1992 and nine in 1993, or in welfare only four and two respectively?

We shall return to possible problems of overload when we discuss the time required for cases to pass through the courts in Chapter 4. For the moment, a further important finding is of the importance of seeing judicial review in its legal context. Thus, a high use of judicial review reflects weaknesses in the availability of other procedures. This is, perhaps, most striking in the case of licensing, where limitations on appeal rights in the Scottish system have resulted in an important category of judicial review which has no counterpart south of the Border. Similarly, the relatively large number of homelessness petitions is the result of the absence of a right of appeal to an independent

---

[29] See *Wordie Property Company Ltd v Secretary of State for Scotland* 1984 SLT 345.
[30] Sections 232–233.

adjudicator in homelessness cases (and it should be recalled that the Dunpark Committee was set up after requests for the establishment of such an appeal right). Indeed, it is possible that the new appeal right in asylum cases from the Immigration Appeal Tribunal on point of law may explain the decrease in judical review petitions concerning immigration in 1994, although there has been a marked increase in 1995. Immigration cases are, however, very different from other petitions, with a large proportion of them, in several years a majority, being designed to gain interim relief rather than a final order.

The implication of viewing judicial review in its legal context in this way is that, should it be felt necessary to limit the number of judicial review petitions brought, the answer lies not in any restrictions such as a leave stage but in providing fuller appeal rights through other procedures in the areas which give rise to the largest numbers of cases, particularly as Scots law shares with English law the principle that alternative remedies must be exhausted before a petition for judicial review becomes competent. Weight is given to this proposition by the absence of homelessness cases in judicial review in Northern Ireland, where the Housing Executive operates a thorough internal review and appeal system.[31] It should be added, however, that much also depends on the quality of the appeal right; otherwise, the provision of an appeal may simply provide a further remedy which needs to be exhausted before applying to the courts. Given the great inconsistency found in the granting of leave by the English courts and the lack of any indication that such a procedure is required to prevent the Court of Session from being overwhelmed by a mass of unarguable cases, the Scots form of procedure has so far proved its worth.

---

[31] 'Trends in Judicial Review in Northern Ireland', *op. cit.*, p 14.

Chapter 4

JUDICIAL REVIEW PROCEDURE

In Chapter 3 we analysed the use made of judicial review and the outcomes of petitions, suggesting that the 1985 procedure had lived up to its promise of facilitating use of judicial review whilst not leading to overwhelming the court's caseload through a large number of hopeless petitions being raised; judicial review was, however, dominated by a relatively small number of subject areas. However, the purpose of the reform in 1985 was not simply to provide a procedure which was accessible; it was to provide a swift procedure, and we also need to examine whether this has been achieved. It will be recalled also from Chapter 2 that some procedural problems remain, in particular those of title and interest to sue, competence and limitations on interim relief. We shall also undertake a brief examination of the degree to which these represent serious difficulties in practice.

The speed of judicial review

Delay in judicial review had become a serious problem in England and Wales by the early 1990s. Thus, in 1991 Lord Justice Woolf compared judicial review to a motorway where:

> [the] tailback, or backlogs, are becoming more and more disturbing. The use of judicial review has grown and is continuing to grow at a pace with which the present structure cannot cope.[1]

The problem was confirmed in the research carried out in England and Wales, which found that of the applications lodged in the first quarter of 1991, one-fifth were completed within 90 days, but three-fifths had not been determined

---
[1] Administrative Law Bar Association Annual Lecture, 4 November 1991, quoted in *Judicial Review in Perspective, op. cit.*, p ix.

within 360 days and 29% took more than 540 days to reach a full hearing.[2] This represented a serious deterioration compared to previous years, although the research did counsel that regard should also be had to the rates of settlement and withdrawal combined with refusals of leave which were not directly affected by these delays.[3]

Since this research was carried out there have been some important developments in England and Wales. Thus, seven extra Queen's Bench judges were appointed in 1993, the number of nominated judges increased from 18 to 23 and a number of other measures taken to develop extra capacity to cope with the caseload problems, such as reducing the number of judges sent out on circuit.[4] This appeared to be successful, with waiting time cut between July 1993 and July 1994 from 21.3 months to 12 months in relation to hearing before a single judge, and from 10.2 months to 7.3 months in relation to hearings before a Divisional Court. It should be noted, however, that this refers not to the time between the lodging of the application and the substantive application, but from entry onto Part B of the Crown Office list (*i.e.* the putting down of cases as ready to be heard after the filing of affidavits and the granting of leave) until the hearing.[5] The Law Commission noted in the response to its consultation paper that:

> [t]here was widespread and almost universal condemnation of the scale of the delays. The period of delay before a non-expedited substantive hearing were variously described as 'completely unacceptable', 'intolerable', 'reaching scandalous proportions', and 'likely to defeat the purpose of taking proceedings'. The nominated judges said that they disfigure the present image of judicial review.[6]

The Commission recommended that the caseload problems be eased by the creation of a right of appeal to a court or independent tribunal in homelessness cases. It also proposed the setting of targets such as a maximum of five-and-a-half months between entry on Part B and the hearing date, and an overall target of nine months from receipt of the application to final disposal.[7]

The earlier Scottish research had found that the speed of disposal was impressive:

> The single most striking feature of the procedure which emerged from our study was its speed. Of the 77 petitions examined, 63 proceeded to a final interlocutor within the period covered. Of these 16 (25 per cent) were disposed of within four weeks, 31 (49 per cent) within six weeks and 43 (68 per cent) within two months of being raised. Only two were not disposed of within six months of being raised. Insofar as one of the main objectives of reform was to expedite the disposal of applications for judicial review, the evidence of our study suggests that it has been outstandingly successful.[8]

---

[2] *Ibid.*, p 59 and information supplied by the Public Law Project.
[3] *Ibid.*, p 60.
[4] *Administrative Law: Judicial Review and Statutory Appeals, op. cit.*, para 2.21.
[5] *Ibid.*, para 2.22 and App 7.
[6] *Ibid.*, para 2.15.
[7] *Ibid.*, App C, paras 8.2–8.3.

4 JUDICIAL REVIEW PROCEDURE

The procedural length in days of cases in this study is set out in Table 1 as a distribution by disposal each 50 days, broken down further by subject.

Table 2 sets out an analysis of minimum, maximum and average disposal times by subject.

In all cases, days means all days including weekends and holidays. Time recorded is from receipt of petition to order. Where there is a settlement the petition will be dismissed or granted and that is used as the end date; this may exaggerate lengths as the effective settlement date may be earlier.

The average is set out at the beginning of Table 2 and at first sight appears to be longer than would be expected from earlier research and, indeed, from our distribution table. Nevertheless, the overall average of 238.93 days is equivalent to about eight months, so beating the English target of nine months. However, the statistics are distorted by a number of factors. First, as is apparent from the distribution table, there is the presence of some cases with extremely long delays, notably two with 2149 days and 2055 days commenced in 1989 and 1990 respectably. These were both immigration cases and it is striking that in every year the times taken for such cases are longer than the average (in 1993 very markedly so). This reflects the fact that in many immigration cases the main objective was interim liberation rather than a final interlocutor, so that they remain inactively on the books for a considerable time. If immigration cases are disregarded, as in Table 2a, the average is a mere 152.83 days. It is also noticeable that the 1993 delay is noticeably lower, reflecting a much quicker disposal of immigration cases commenced in that year, although this may be due to the relative lack of cases left on the books for very long periods in that year. Taking all cases, including immigration, together, an average time for disposal of six-and-a-half months in 1993 cases is much more impressive than the overall average for all years suggests; it is the lowest average in any of the years studied. It

Table 4.1 Distribution of disposal by days

	All Years	1988	1989	1990	1991	1992	1993
Up to 50 days	120	20	33	10	22	15	20
51–100 days	88	8	9	14	15	22	20
101–150 days	65	7	8	7	5	15	23
151–200 days	38	3	0	6	3	9	17
201–250 days	29	1	3	5	4	4	12
251–300 days	23	0	0	3	3	8	9
301–500 days	71	4	8	5	12	18	24
501–1000 days	35	7	4	7	6	7	4
1001 and over	19	7	9	0	1	2	0
9999 (Out of Court)	71	9	12	5	7	17	21
Total	559*	66	86	62	78	117	150*

*Excludes one case still live at the completion of the study.

[8] 'Judicial Review in the Court of Session', op. cit., p 62.

Table 4.2 Length until disposal by days and by subject

	1988	1989	1990	1991	1992	1993	1988-93
All cases	66	86	62	78	117	151	560
Average	347.77	295.12	213.61	204.24	230.33	195.54	238.93
Minimum	3	2	7	3	2	8	2
Maximum	2149	2055	981	1034	1039	735	2149
Immigration cases	15	21	12	17	36	55	156
Average	950.69	880.95	363.75	481.80	395.67	200.37	450.81
Minimum	10	5	35	7	38	9	5
Maximum	2149	2055	981	1034	1039	570	2149
Housing cases	8	10	9	10	26	26	89
Average	236.86	231	147.89	176.56	176.24	180.82	185.69
Minimum	26	30	11	37	31	38	11
Maximum	675	417	233	414	401	538	675
Licensing cases	8	28	7	13	11	25	92
Average	248.86	35.91	211	48.58	70.56	248.45	134.38
Minimum	3	2	25	8	39	16	2
Maximum	905	86	766	113	107	463	905
Planning cases	8	7	10	8	8	5	46
Average	90.83	87	152.22	140.14	78.6	95.75	113.35
Minimum	13	16	39	45	38	53	13
Maximum	190	210	338	310	143	141	338
All other cases	27	20	24	30	36	39*	176*
Average	146.63	95	183.05	147.18	162.21	174.38	154.41
Minimum	15	23	7	3	2	8	2
Maximum	589	633	886	571	488	735	886

* Excludes one case as still live at completion of the study.

Table 4.2a Length until disposal excluding immigration cases

	1988	1989	1990	1991	1992	1993	1988-93
All Cases (excluding immigration)	51	65	50	61	81	95*	403*
Average	169.64	92.75	173.58	129.89	148.9	189.23	152.83
Minimum	3	2	7	3	2	8	2
Maximum	905	633	886	571	488	735	905

*Excludes one case as still live at completition of the study.

should also be noted that some cases in the study have been disposed of exceptionally quickly; thus, in each year, the minimum number of days has been in single figures. This could represent hopeless cases abandoned quickly or strong cases taken by an expedited procedure. In fact, both seem to exist; of 34 cases determined within 20 days, 20 were determined by refusal to grant the petition, but in five cases the petition was granted in full and in five others it was granted in part. The speed of the very quickest cases was particularly striking; in two successful petitions the disposal took only two days, intimation and service having been dispensed with.

Turning to the individual subjects, the peculiarities of immigration cases have been noted above. In housing, the overall average time for disposal was a little over six months. This may seem to be lengthy given that a large proportion of the cases concern homelessness and so appear extremely urgent. However, the position is complicated here also by the potential complexity of objectives and disposal. The main aim in such cases might be interim relief and, as we saw in Chapter 3, housing cases had a particularly high settlement rate; early settlement may not be reflected in the figures for the length of cases set out in our tables. Once more, there is a very great difference between the minimum and maximum times for disposal, again suggesting that a part is played by settled cases or those in which interim relief is granted remaining on the books. This would suggest that even taking the category of homelessness cases alone, disposal times are much quicker than the overall average would suggest.

Licensing cases present quite a different pattern. Here, there is a particularly radical variation between the overall average of all cases and those in particular years. Thus, the year in which the largest number of such petitions was brought (1989, with 28) had an average disposal time of only a little over one month; 1991 and 1992 also produced very quick disposals. By contrast, 1993, with 25 petitions, had a long disposal time of over eight months (this was due to a number of cases being brought concerning the Glasgow licensing curfew which were sisted whilst a test case was determined; the cases then remained on the books for a considerable period, once more exaggerating the overall length).[9]

Planning cases were relatively low in number and here the average disposal time was markedly shorter, at less than four months; this is increased by the longer average times in 1990–91, and for 1993 the time is only a little over three months. The remaining miscellaneous cases show a large deviation between minimum, average and maximum times and, again, the effect of cases left on the books but inactive will have influenced this; as they are variegated they do not yield useful information on the effects of the procedure in meeting the need for quick decisions.

On the basis of the bare statistics, it would seem that the times taken for the disposal of cases are longer than those found in the earlier Page research quoted above. However, for a number of reasons this is misleading. First, there is the effect of the large numbers of cases which lie inactively on the books; these will be particularly important in immigration, after the granting of interim relief, and in other areas (especially housing), where a settlement has been reached. Thus, the statistics in themselves are of limited use in determining the real effects of delay or the lack of it. A more accurate picture can be drawn from the distribution pattern in Table 1, although even this exaggerates the length of cases due to the effect of cases left on the books after the granting of interim relief and early settlements. Nevertheless, even on the basis of this limited data which systematically overstates the time taken for the disposal of cases, two conclusions can be drawn. First, the serious delays associated with the

---

[9] The test case was *Cinderella's Rockafella's v Glasgow District Licensing Board* 1994 SCLR 591.

increase in caseload in the English judicial review procedure have not been repeated in Scotland. Thus, even the uncorrected data taking no account of interim relief and settlement patterns give an overall time which is better than the **target** proposed by the Law Commission, let alone recent practice. Secondly, the figures for the speed of handling cases, even on an uncorrected basis, show that the procedure is quicker than that for other types of civil procedure. Thus, recent work on personal injury litigation found that the average length between tabling and final disposal in the Court of Session was 18 months under ordinary procedure and nine months under the simplified optional procedure.[10] It should also be stressed that there is no evidence of a general slowing down of the procedure; the average time for 1993 is the lowest in any year of our study, and every year since 1988 (except for 1992) has seen a lessening of the average disposal time. Disposal of more than half of the 1993 petitions in less than 200 days is a highly creditable achievement. In view of these findings we can only reiterate the finding of the earlier Scottish study that, in terms of speed, the 1985 reform had been outstandingly successful.

Effects of the lack of a leave filter

As we are now discussing procedural issues, it will be useful to bring together some of the implications of our study for the absence of a requirement of leave on the model of that which exists elsewhere in the United Kingdom. What are the purposes of this filter? In relation to England and Wales, the Law Commission stated the purpose of this filter succinctly:

> [t]he purpose of the requirement in Order 53 that no application for judicial review shall be made unless the leave of the Court has been obtained is to filter out hopeless applications. Ill-founded applications delay finality in decision-making: they exploit and exacerbate delays within the judicial system and are detrimental to the progress of well-founded legal challenges. While this is generally true of litigation, in the case of applications challenging regulations and decisions ... public policy factors ... have been seen as justifying the filter provided by the present leave requirement.[11]

The public policy reasons for leave include the need for speed and certainty in administrative decision-making in cases where the whole community, or large sections of it, will be affected by the decisions of public law bodies. On the other hand, the English research established that there were very wide inconsistencies in the approach to leave decisions by different judges and that 'there is a substantial risk that potentially arguable applications are being prematurely rejected. In particular, our data have highlighted both the uncertain nature of the leave hurdle and the considerable variation in approach amongst the

---
[10] G Cameron, with R Johnston, *Personal Injury Litigation in the Scottish Courts: A Descriptive Analysis* (Scottish Office Central Research Unit, 1995), para 6.8.
[11] *Administrative Law: Judicial Review and Statutory Appeals, op. cit.*, para 5.1; see also para 2.3.

judges'.[12] The Law Commission considered that it was essential to filter out hopeless applications by a requirement such as leave in order to retain a broad judicial discretion, although it should be renamed 'preliminary consideration'.[13] In Northern Ireland a simpler procedure for leave applies and it may be granted by a Master rather than a judge; in 1991, for example, over 60% of leave decisions were taken on the day of lodging or the following day.[14]

None of these arguments would appear to support the introduction of a leave requirement in Scotland. We saw in Chapter 3 that there is no evidence to suggest that the Court of Session is being overwhelmed by a mass of hopeless cases; even in the fastest-growing category of immigration cases it appeared that the granting of interim relief in a large number of cases suggested that the judicial review procedure was performing an important function in providing quick review of detention which would not otherwise be available, and the high rate of grant of relief suggested that these cases were not in any sense an abuse of the court's process which should have been filtered out. It has now been established that the lack of a leave requirement has not led to serious delays in the court; even the interpretation of the figures, which fails to correct for considerations such as the effect of settlements and cases still on the books after interim relief, shows times for disposal which beat even the targets proposed for the English High Court. The discretion of the judge in the process should be sufficient to dispose of any weak cases quickly at the hearing; this seems to be confirmed by the existence of a number of quick disposals (in less than 20 days) in which the petition was dismissed. Should there be any increase in petitions in the future which threatens the smooth handling of cases, we shall make other recommendations for dealing with the problem in our conclusion, through the creation of other remedies for cases now exclusively within the judicial review procedure. Quite simply, there is no ground to suggest the importation of a requirement for the granting of leave.

Expenses and legal aid

A further justification for the introduction of the 1985 procedure for judicial review was that it would be cheap; Lord Fraser had, indeed, referred to a procedure which would be 'speedy and cheap' in his speech in *Brown v Hamilton District Council*,[15] which had been the main impetus for reform. Table 3 sets out the expenses figures for those cases (about one-third of all in the study) for which a detailed award of expenses could be found in the case documentation.

The question of accessibility to judicial review and the problem of costs will be examined in more detail in out adviser survey in Chapter 6. At this stage it

---
[12] *Judicial Review in Perspective, op. cit.*, Ch 6 and p 102; see also 'Applications for Judicial Review: The Requirement of Leave', *op. cit.*
[13] *Administrative Law: Judicial Review and Statutory Appeals, op. cit.*, Part V.
[14] 'Trends in Judicial Review in Northern Ireland', *op. cit.*, p 13.
[15] 1983 SLT 397 at 418.

Table 4.3 Expenses

Expenses	Number	Percentage
Up to £1000	12	11.10%
Between £1001 and £2000	42	38.90%
Between £2001 and £3000	23	21.30%
Between £3001 and £5000	15	13.90%
Over £5001	16	14.80%
Total	108	100.00%

Cost information for judicial review (not including the cost of appeal) was given in 108 cases. Expenses were awarded in 313 cases. In the remaining 247 cases, no expenses were awarded, expenses were not mentioned, or the case was otherwise taken out of court. Information on the amount of expenses was available for only 108 of the 313 cases (34.5%), in which expenses were awarded.

Table 4.4 Legal aid for individual petitioners

	1	2	3	4	5	Total
1988	25	14	3	0	0	42
	59.5%	33.3%	7.1%	0.0%	0.0%	99.9%
1989	25	23	0	0	0	48
	52.1%	47.9%	0.0%	0.0%	0.0%	100.0%
1990	22	12	3	0	0	37
	59.5%	32.4%	8.1%	0.0%	0.0%	100.0%
1991	27	18	1	0	0	46
	58.7%	39.1%	2.2%	0.0%	0.0%	100.0%
1992	41	40	2	0	0	83
	49.4%	48.2%	2.4%	0.0%	0.0%	100.0%
1993	51	46	6	2	2	107
	47.7%	43.0%	5.6%	1.9%	1.9%	100.1%
1988–93	191	153	15	2	2	363
	52.6%	42.1%	4.1%	0.6%	0.6%	100.0%

Explanation of coding: 1 = has legal aid; 2 = no legal aid; 3 = applied for during process and unclear as to result; 4 = applied for during process and refused; 5 = applied for during process and granted.

can be said that the procedure is apparently relatively cheap, with half the awards of expenses at £2000 or below.

Although legal aid in judicial review proceedings will be discussed fully in Chapter 5, it is convenient to provide an indication of its role in the procedure here.

It will be seen that legal aid had been awarded in about half of the judicial review cases brought by individual petitioners. Not surprisingly, there was a strong difference by subject-matter; this is set out in Table 5, with statistics based on all petitions to give an overall view.

Thus, legal aid was granted in over 75% of housing petitions; the proportion

Table 4.5 Legal aid by subject: all petitions

Subject	1	2	3	4	5	Total
Housing	71 79.8%	15 16.9%	0 0%	1 1.1%	2 2.2%	89 100%
Immigration	59 37.8%	84 53.8%	12 7.7%	1 0.6%	0 0%	156 99.9%
Licensing	3 3.3%	89 96.7%	0 0%	0 0%	0 0%	92 100%
Planning & land use	2 4.3%	44 95.7%	0 0%	0 0%	0 0%	46 100%
All other subjects	56 31.6%	118 66.7%	3 1.7%	0 0%	0 0%	177 100%
Total	191 34.1%	350 62.5%	15 2.7%	2 0.4%	2 0.4%	560 100.1%

Explanation of coding: 1 = has legal aid; 2 = no legal aid; 3 = applied for during process and unclear as to result; 4 = applied for during process and refused; 5 = applied for during process and granted.

for immigration varied between 27% in 1993 and 71% in 1989 on a much smaller number of petitions. The grant of legal aid in immigration cases declined steadily from 1989–93. Fuller analysis of legal aid and its award will take place in Chapter 5.

Use of nominated judges

It will be recalled that a recommendation of the Dunpark Committee was that English practice should be adopted through the creation of 'a panel of nominated judges [which] would enable those Judges to develop an expertise in this branch of the law and with this procedure which should produce a greater consistency than casual allotment to any available judge'.[16] This was implemented in the new procedure, although if such a judge was not available the petition was to be heard by any other judge. The English research established that judges other than those on the nominated list were extensively involved in judicial review decisions. Thus, in the period 1987–92 a total of 32 judges were on the list at some time; however, a total of 70 judges were involved in decisions on cases begun in 1987, 78 on cases begun in 1988, and 75 in cases initiated in the first quarter of 1991.[17] Even amongst the ranks of the nominated judges, there were very large inconsistencies in the patterns of leave decisions reached.

Table 6 sets out some information on the use of nominated judges. It will be seen that there has been a considerable decline in the proportion of cases in

---
[16] Dunpark Report, *op. cit.*, commentary on r 2.
[17] *Judicial Review in Perspective, op. cit.*, p 83.

Table 4.6 Use of nominated judges

	Number of nominated judges at first hearing	Percentage of all hearings
1988	31	91.2%
1989	33	80.5%
1990	24	70.6%
1991	21	52.5%
1992	27	67.5%
1993	28	56.0%
1988–93	164	68.6%

For first hearings we also include those cases where there was a hearing on the interim orders. There were three in the entire time period.

which the first hearing was held by a nominated judge; indeed, in 1991 and 1993 only a little more than half the hearings were held before such a judge. The only year in which the decline was stemmed to some extent was 1992, although this did not last. The further fall in the proportion of such hearings in 1993 is hardly surprising given the large increase in petitions in that year. It will be recalled that one response in England to the dramatic rise in caseload and the ensuing delays was to increase the number of nominated judges from 18 to 23; in Scotland, since the period of the research, the number of nominated judges has been increased from five to six, although the need for speed means that urgent cases must still go to other judges. On the one hand, a situation where only half of first hearings are before nominated judges risks losing those elements of special expertise stressed by the Dunpark Committee as quoted above. On the other hand, our data does not suggest that there are strong inconsistencies between nominated and non-nominated judges in the outcomes of petitions; indeed, outcomes appear remarkably consistent, and in the 238 cases which reached a first hearing, the petition was granted in full or in part in 38.5% of the petitions where there was a first hearing before a nominated judge and in 41.9% of those before another judge (this excludes, of course, cases settled before the first hearing and cases taken out of court). This could be explained by the fact that judicial review in Scotland is confined to full-time judges and petitions are not heard by temporary judges, whilst in England part-time judges do hear judicial review cases.[18] The number of petitions is too small for a statistically meaningful analysis to be undertaken of variations in decision-making by individual judges.

Interim relief

A brief summary of the role of interim relief in judicial review was given in Chapters 2 and 3. It will be recalled that the rules of court make provision for

---

[18] The researchers are grateful to the Lord President for information on this issue.

4 JUDICIAL REVIEW PROCEDURE

the granting of such relief, although a problem has been the lack of availability of coercive remedies (notably interim injunction in England, interim interdict in Scotland) against the Crown. This problem has been remedied to some degree through recent decisions in England, but not in Scotland (except as regards the protection of rights derived from European Community law).[19] In England, interim relief is sought in about 10% of cases, particularly homelessness cases where interim relief is almost always sought.[20] The Law Commission has recommended that in England the rules of court should be amended to make it clear that there is jurisdiction to grant interim relief before the grant of leave, and that specific authority should be granted for the making of interim injunctions, interim declarations and stays of proceedings.[21]

Statistics on the role of interim relief in Scotland are set out in Table 7, which deals only with those cases in which interim relief was requested.

It appears that overall interim relief was requested in over half the petitions for judicial review. In about one-third of cases in which such relief was requested relief was refused outright; in a further 8% the request was not considered by the court, and in 10% it was not granted, but an undertaking was instead given to the court. By far the most common form of interim relief was interim liberation, granted in one-quarter of cases where interim relief was requested, underlining the key role of such relief in immigration cases; thus, in immigration cases interim relief (in the vast majority of cases interim liberation) was requested in over 80% of cases. Moreover, in 75% of cases in which interim liberation was requested, it was granted.[22] The second largest category for such relief was interim interdict, granted in 6.5% of cases in which interim relief was requested. This covered a range of different subject areas, including planning, homelessness and licencing. In the case of homelessness, however, the most common relief sought was an order to secure accommodation, which was granted in 12 cases during the whole study; in eight such cases no order was made but an undertaking was given at bar.

To underline our findings in Chapter 3, in immigration cases the very extensive use of interim liberation is a Scottish peculiarity, which in effect, amounts to the use of judicial review as a bail application. It is influenced by the other Scottish peculiarity of the 110-day rule in the criminal process which creates a greater propensity to grant relief and which also prevents long periods of detention in immigration cases, as described in Chapter 3. It is important that any proposals for change in Scottish judicial review takes account of this important and unique function of the procedure; it is a further reason why English experience is not a good guide to Scottish needs.

---

[19] *McDonald v Secretary of State for Scotland* 1994 SLT 692.
[20] *Administrative Law: Judicial Review and Statutory Appeals, op. cit.*, para 4.4.
[21] *Ibid.*, Part VI.
[22] See Chapter 3, Table 10 for details.

Table 4.7 Interim relief outcomes

	1988	1989	1990	1991	1992	1993	Total
0	13 29.50%	11 27.50%	12 40.00%	18 42.90%	21 30.00%	32 38.10%	107 34.50%
1	3 6.80%	3 7.50%	2 6.70%	3 7.10%	5 7.10%	4 4.80%	20 6.50%
2	2 4.50%	3 7.50%	3 10.00%	3 7.10%	2 2.90%	1 1.20%	14 4.50%
3	9 20.50%	13 32.50%	6 20.00%	5 11.90%	17 24.30%	30 35.70%	80 25.80%
4	0 0.00%	2 5.00%	1 3.30%	1 2.40%	4 5.70%	6 7.10%	14 4.50%
5	0 0.00%	1 2.50%	0 0.00%	0 0.00%	0 0.00%	0 0.00%	1 0.30%
6	0 0.00%	0 0.00%	0 0.00%	0 0.00%	0 0.00%	0 0.00%	0 0.00%
7	0 0.00%	0 0.00%	0 0.00%	0 0.00%	2 2.90%	0 0.00%	2 0.60%
8	3 6.80%	4 10.00%	5 16.70%	5 11.90%	7 10.00%	8 9.50%	32 10.30%
9	22 N/A	48 N/A	32 N/A	36 N/A	47 N/A	67 N/A	252 N/A
10	2 4.50%	0 0.00%	0 0.00%	0 0.00%	2 2.90%	1 1.20%	5 1.60%
11	12 27.3%	1 2.50%	1 3.30%	5 11.9%	6 8.60%	0 0.00%	25 8.10%
12	0 0.00%	0 0.00%	0 0.00%	2 4.8%	2 2.90%	0 0.00%	4 1.30%
13	0 0.00%	2 5.00%	0 0.00%	0 0.00%	2 2.90%	2 2.40%	6 1.90%
All	44	40	30	42	70	84	310

Explanation of coding: 0 = not granted; 1 = interdict; 2 = suspension; 3 = liberation; 4 = order/decree/implement; 5 = interdict and suspension; 6 = interdict and liberation; 7 = interdict and order/implement; 8 = not granted but undertaking given at bar; 9 = not requested; 10 = granted but withdrawn; 11 = not considered; 12 = other; 13 = liberation and suspension.

Title and interest to sue

A problem which might limit the utility of the judicial review procedure is the restrictive and confused nature of the law relating to standing (termed title and interest to sue) in Scotland. In England and Wales there has been progress since the introduction of the new procedure under RSC Order 53 for both the widening and simplification of standing in judicial review.[23] Thus, the new English Order referred to the need to show a 'sufficient interest', and this has generally been interpreted liberally, reflecting the liberal position applying to the prerogative orders before 1977.[24] This has not been a wholly consistent trend, and some doubts have remained as to the nature and role of the standing requirement.[25] The initial reasons for the reluctance to widen standing have been eased by the inclusion of the 'sufficient interest' requirement in the Supreme Court Act 1981,[26] so making it clear that even if standing is a matter of substantive law, liberalisation could have been effective, and recent caselaw has taken a much more generous approach to applications by pressure groups.[27] The Law Commission recommended that a test be adopted of asking whether the applicant has been or would be adversely affected, or, alternatively, whether it is in the public interest for the applicant to make the application.[28]

In Scotland, the law is complex, requiring tests both of legal title and interest to be satisfied.[29] The law is potentially highly restrictive in relation to petitions by business competitors, by third parties in planning and by pressure groups.[30] The Dunpark Committee (differing from the views of the Faculty of Advocates in this respect) considered that standing was a matter of substantive law which could not competently be changed by Act of Sederunt and so did not include a reformed test of standing in its proposals. Nevertheless, it stated that '[t]here is, in our opinion, a strong case for the extension by the legislature of our common law rules of title and interest to sue to enable every person who is directly or indirectly affected by alleged unlawful acts or decisions competently to challenge them'.[31] The legislature has not taken up the invitation, but there have been signs of a more liberal approach in some of the reported cases.[32] This has not, however, been wholly consistent, with business competitors still being held not to possess title and interest in some reported cases.[33]

The more generous approach was noted in the earlier Scottish research, which found that no cases were refused simply because of lack of standing, including cases brought by third parties and competitors in planning and

---

[23] For the current position in England, see P Craig, *Administrative Law*, 3rd ed. Sweet & Maxwell, (1994), Ch 13.
[24] *Administrative Law: Judicial Review and Statutory Appeals, op. cit.*, para 5.17.
[25] See, *e.g.*, *R v Environment Secretary ex parte Rose Theatre Trust Company* [1990] 1 QB 504; *IRC v National Federation of Self Employed* [1982] AC 617.
[26] Section 31(3).
[27] *R v HM Inspectorate of Pollution ex parte Greenpeace* [1994] 1 WLR 570; *R v Secretary of State for Foreign and Commonwealth Affairs ex parte World Development Movement Ltd* [1995] 1 All ER 611.
[28] *Administrative Law: Judicial Review and Statutory Appeals, op. cit.*, para 5.22.
[29] *Stair Memorial Encyclopedia: The Laws of Scotland*, 'Administrative Law' (Butterworths), paras 308–323.
[30] *D and J Nichol v Dundee Harbour Trustees* 1915 SC 7 (HL); *Simpson v Edinburgh Corporation and Edinburgh University* 1960 SC 313; *Scottish Old People's Welfare Council, Petitioners* 1987 SLT 179.
[31] Paragraph 8.
[32] See, *e.g.*, *Lakin Ltd v Secretary of State for Scotland* 1988 SLT 780 (IH); *Kincardine and Deeside District Council v Forestry Commissioners* 1992 SLT 1180, and cases referred to in n 35 below.
[33] *Matchett v Dunfermline District Council* 1993 SLT 537; *Hollywood Bowl (Scotland) Ltd v Horsburgh* 1993 SLT 241.

licensing cases; the point on standing was not raised or not pressed, and respondents appeared to prefer to concentrate on the merits of the petition.[34] In our research we also found that a more generous approach to title and interest was taken, in practice, than the more restrictive reported cases would suggest. Although, as we described in Chapter 3, we did not find a pure pressure group action brought on behalf of non-members, such as the World Development Movement litigation in England, there were several examples of petitions by business competitors and by third parties in planning cases without problems of title and interest having been raised;[35] nor did the adviser survey suggest that there were concerns about standing, although those interviewed were all acting for individual clients rather than pressure groups. If, in practice, title and interest requirements have become more relaxed than the older cases would suggest, this should be recognised more formally; given the potential problems of amendment by Act of Sederunt and the lack of likelihood of legislative change, a definitive statement by the court of the relevant principles would seem appropriate. After all, the more restrictive formal rules are themselves the product of judicial decision.

Competence

Reference was also made in Chapter 2 to the question of when, and against which bodies, the judicial review procedure is available. It will be recalled that considerable difficulties had arisen in England with the assertion of procedural exclusivity by the House of Lords in *O'Reilly v Mackman*,[36] and the distinction between rights protected under public law and those protected under private law. In Scotland, the judicial review procedure had been made exclusive in the sense of being the only procedure for applications to the supervisory jurisdiction of the court, but this, of course, begs the question of which cases involve such applications. After some importation of the English test, it was roundly rejected by the First Division in *West v Secretary of State for Scotland*,[37] stating that the cases in which the exercise of the supervisory jurisdiction is appropriate involve a tripartite relationship.

This could have two possible implications for the use of judicial review. On the one hand, the repudiation of the public/private distinction might seem to open the way to challenge of bodies and functions which do not fall into traditional notions of the public sector; one example would be arbiters, clearly

---

[34] 'Judicial Review in the Court of Session', *op. cit.*, pp 60–61; see also 'Comments on the Paper by A Page', *ibid.*, p 67.
[35] For reported examples, see *Lothian Health Board v City of Edinburgh District Council and J Sainsbury plc* 1992 SCLR 431 (business competitor); *James Aitken and Sons v City of Edinburgh District Council and Link Housing Association* 1990 SLT 241 (neighbour); and *Trusthouse Forte UK Ltd v Perth and Kinross District Council and Flicks (Scotland) Ltd* 1990 SLT 737 (neighbour).
[36] [1981] 2 AC 237.
[37] 1992 SLT 636; see also *Joobeen v University of Stirling* 1995 SLT 120 and *Blair v Lochaber District Council* 1995 SLT 407.

reviewable on the basis of *West* and, indeed, of earlier authority.[38] On the other hand, the nature of the required 'tripartite relationship' has been doubted and may be in need of clarification.[39]

Our research does not analyse in detail cases after 1993 and so cannot provide a full indication of any possible effects of the *West* decision. Nevertheless, to repeat a point made in the survey of respondents in Chapter 3, the range of bodies against which judicial review has been sought has been wide. Examples in our study have included not only a wide range of public sector bodies, including health boards, the Traffic Commissioner, the Scottish Legal Aid Board and universities, but also a number of examples outside the traditional public sector, such as arbiters. Once more, it seems that the formal rules about competence have caused little problem in practice, and there is no question of the judicial review procedure being overwhelmed by cases more appropriately brought by other means.

Damages

A further matter of controversy south of the Border has been the availability of damages in judicial review. This raises important and complex issues of administrative liability. We will restrict ourselves here to an examination of the procedural issues involved. In England, damages are available, in principle, in judicial review proceedings if they could have been awarded in ordinary civil proceedings, but their award is, in practice, rare. In Scotland, the Dunpark Committee recommended that damages and restitution could be sought as ancillary remedies, and noted that they might be appropriate in, for example, some homeless persons cases.[40] Rule 58.4 of the RCS explicitly permits the award of damages as the judge thinks fit (damages were awarded in one reported homelessness case).[41] However, in no case in our sample were damages actually rewarded in judicial review proceedings, although in a number of cases damages were requested in the petition.

Conclusions

Great stress was placed in the Dunpark Report on the need for a judicial review procedure which was both speedy and flexible. Our research suggests that these objectives have been substantially achieved. Despite the increase in caseload, judicial review remains a quick procedure; notably, the heavy delays and other caseload problems which have occurred in the English jurisdiction have not

---

[38] *Forbes v Underwood* (1886) 13 R 465.
[39] *Naik v University of Stirling* 1994 SLT 449; but *cf. Blair v Lochaber District Council* 1995 SLT 407 in which some clarification was given.
[40] *Op. cit.*, commentary on draft rule 4.
[41] *Kelly v Monklands District Council* 1986 SLT 169 at 173.

been a problem in Scotland. The flexibility of the procedure remains a big advantage, permitting, for example, a relatively generous approach to be taken to interim relief and the apparently strict rules on standing to be applied more generously in practice. There is no sign of the sort of overloading of the procedure which would justify the introduction of a leave requirement. It should be stressed once more that judicial review also has a unique role in immigration cases as a form of disguised bail application through the request of interim liberation; the success rate of such petitions is high at the interim stage and the importance of this role for the procedure should not be underestimated. Some problems remain in other aspects of judicial review (for example, the decline in the proportion of cases which are heard by nominated judges). However, this has not created the problems of inconsistency so evident in England. Another problem is the continuing uncertainty over the standing rules which, whilst less of a problem in practice than in theory, may deter potential applicants, a question which will be addressed more fully in our analysis of the adviser survey below.

It could be argued that speed and flexibility are, however, a relative luxury permitted by the limited use of judicial review in Scotland. It was also suggested in Chapter 3 that judicial review was underused in areas of public administration other than homelessness and immigration. We will now assess whether there are barriers outside the procedure which limit the number of petitions raised, commencing with a study of legal aid decisions and then analysing the role, and views, of legal and lay advisers.

Chapter 5

LEGAL AID AND JUDICIAL REVIEW

Introduction

A high proportion of those seeking judicial review do so with the benefit of legal aid. Over the whole period covered by our research, 34.5% of petitioners were legally aided.[1] If cases in which the petitioner was a corporate body or an individual pursuing a trading interest are excluded, the proportion of legally aided petitioners rises to 53.2%.[2] The expansion of judicial review since 1985 has, therefore, been heavily reliant on public funding of litigants. However, the significance of legal aid is twofold: not only does it pay for representation that an individual would not otherwise be able to afford, the grant of legal aid also makes it extremely unlikely that the unsuccessful petitioner will have to pay legal expenses. A significant proportion of respondents do not ask for expenses against unsuccessful legally aided petitioners. In addition, where expenses are awarded against a legally aided person, there is provision, which is frequently used, for expenses to be modified to nil.[3]

If, in these two ways, legal aid facilitates access to judicial review, it also functions as a barrier. Where legal aid is refused, the petitioner is unlikely to go on to lodge a petition for judicial review. Legal aid, therefore, operates as a filter. Given the statutory conditions which must be satisfied before legal aid can be granted, it should screen out cases which lack legal merit, or which are not appropriate for support from public funds. It is of fundamental importance that this filter operates properly, neither screening out worthwhile cases, nor funding worthless cases.

---

[1] See Table 5 in Chapter 4, at p 49. The proportion legally aided in particular years was highest in 1988 at 37.9% and lowest in 1989 at 28.4 %. In subsequent years there is little deviation from the mean.

[2] See Table 4 in Chapter 4, at p 48.

[3] See the Legal Aid (Scotland) Act 1986, s 18(2), and CN Stoddart and H Neilson, *The Law and Practice of Legal Aid in Scotland*, 4th ed (T & T Clark, 1994), at 14–06–14–25.

Legal aid is clearly an important factor influencing access to judicial review, but by no means the only one. The legal aid filter will tend to have a markedly different impact in the various areas of substantive law which give rise to applications for judicial review. It seems sensible to make a broad distinction between the fields of commercial law and welfare law: by the former we mean the areas in which litigation is dominated by commercial interests, for example the various kinds of licensing, and town and country planning; by the latter we mean the areas in which litigation is begun primarily by private individuals not asserting trading interests, for example, housing, immigration control, social security, and education. In the commercial law area most litigants are not legally aided. In the areas we describe as welfare law, most litigants do obtain legal aid.

We attempted to find out more about the factors influencing access to review through a survey of legal and lay advisers.[4] We doubted whether there was a significant problem of access to judicial review for commercial clients. It seems reasonable to suppose that access to judicial review operates somewhat differently in the context of commercial cases and in the context of welfare law cases.[5] Our main concern was to investigate factors influencing access to review in the welfare law field, and the solicitors and advisers interviewed were chosen accordingly. Accordingly, we have a great deal to say about access to judicial review in the welfare law field, but little to say about access to review in the context of commercial law.

We considered that a detailed study of legal aid decision-making might shed light on a number of issues relevant to the research, including the relationship between the actual number of judicial reviews and the potential for judicial review, the way in which legal aid affects access to review, and the extent to which, and the way in which, disputes are settled without resulting in applications for review. It was originally our intention to conduct a detailed analysis of legal aid decision-making involving scrutiny of legal aid files, and interviews of those taking decisions. However, it proved difficult to surmount the statutory confidentiality provisions[6] and, in the event, a more limited study was undertaken. The Scottish Legal Aid Board kindly provided detailed statistical information in response to a series of questions framed by us. These were followed up by discussions with officials, and exchanges of correspondence in the course of which further information was supplied. A number of the legal and lay advisers interviewed in the later stages of the project also made comments about legal aid which contributed to our understanding of its role in judicial review.

The original research design proposed examining the following issues: the time taken to make decisions on the award of legal aid; the operation of the

---

[4] See Chapter 6.
[5] If our assumption that there is not a problem of access to review for commercial clients is incorrect, this is a matter that future research could cover.
[6] Section 34 of the Legal Aid (Scotland) Act 1986 prohibits, subject to certain exceptions, disclosure of any information supplied in connection with an application for legal aid without the consent of the applicant.

review procedure; the way in which the legal requirements for the grant of legal aid are applied; and the nature and extent of the documentation required for a successful application, together with solicitors' abilities to provide them. Despite not having access to the files, the information which we have been able to obtain makes a significant, albeit incomplete, contribution to understanding these issues. The most important limitation of the research is that we were not able directly to examine and evaluate either the quality of legal aid decision-making in individual cases, or the quality of legal aid applications by solicitors.

The legal aid system

Legal aid in Scotland is governed by the Legal Aid (Scotland) Act 1986 and regulations made thereunder.[7] Administration is the responsibility of the Scottish Legal Aid Board ('the Board'). In order to fund an application for judicial review, an application for civil legal aid under Part III of the Act is made. There are two types of criteria for the award of civil legal aid: financial, and those related to the merits of the application. The financial criteria restrict the availability of legal aid to those whose disposable income and capital fall within certain limits. There are two separate criteria relating to the merits. Civil legal aid is only available:

> if the Board is satisfied that [the applicant] has *probabilis causa litigandi*; and ... it appears to the Board that it is reasonable in the particular circumstances of the case that he should receive legal aid.[8]

Both the financial conditions and the merits tests are administered by the Board.

The expression '*probabilis causa litigandi*' may be translated literally as 'a probable cause for being a party to legal action'. No further interpretation of the term is given in the Act or the regulations, nor has it been the subject of judicial interpretation. The Board has issued a number of guidance notes[9] indicating the sort of information it would expect to see accompanying an application for civil legal aid, which refer to specific types of civil proceeding, for example applications to pursue divorce action. These guidelines give some indication of what it will take to convince the Board that there is probable cause for litigating in the particular contexts to which they refer. There are no guidelines which apply to all civil proceedings, and none of the specific guidelines refer to judicial review.[10] However, in practice in a judicial review case, the Board would expect the application form to be accompanied by a copy of the decision of

---

[7] The principal regulations are the Civil Legal Aid (Scotland) Regulations 1987 (SI 1987 No 381).
[8] Legal Aid (Scotland) Act 1986, s 14(1).
[9] The guidance notes are collected together in *The Scottish Legal Aid Handbook* (Scottish Legal Aid Board, 1992) (2nd ed. in preparation).
[10] At the time of writing the Board is giving consideration to publishing guidelines on applications for legal aid for judicial review.

which review is sought, a statement of the grounds on which review is sought, and precognitions and other documents, where relevant, in order to enable the application to be decided.

Despite the absence of a precise definition of *probabilis causa*, it is clear that, in practice, it can be broken down into two elements: legal and factual. The applicant needs to show that he has grounds in law for raising or defending the legal action for which he is seeking funding. In the context of judicial review, this will mean grounds for arguing that the prospective respondent has acted unlawfully in terms of the principles of judicial review. To satisfy the factual element, the applicant will have to assert that the facts are such as to support the legal argument, and that there are some prospects of being able to prove to a court that the facts are as the applicant asserts. As indicated above, neither the regulations nor the guidance notes indicate how high the probability of convincing the court of the correctness of either the legal or the factual claim needs to be to justify the award of legal aid in the context of judicial review. However, the degree of probability of convincing a court of the soundness of the factual or legal claims will be relevant to the Board's consideration of whether it is reasonable to grant legal aid in the circumstances.

Neither the Act, the regulations, nor the guidance notes amplify the reasonableness test. However, there is limited guidance in the caselaw. In *McColl v Strathclyde Regional Council*[11] an elderly woman was granted legal aid to petition to interdict the local authority from adding fluoride to the water supply. The petition was successful, but Lord Jauncey doubted whether the legal aid legislation was intended to achieve the effect that the petitioner 'had been placed in a position far superior to that of a normal person litigating at his own expense ...'.[12] Lord Jauncey considered that only an individual with unlimited means could have afforded to pursue the litigation, and doubted whether even such an individual would have considered it worthwhile to embark on the case. These *dicta* provide support for the Board's practice of not, in general, granting applications for proceedings which a private client would not pursue.

Stoddart and Neilson suggest that applications may be turned down on grounds of reasonableness, *inter alia*, where the application is one in which many members of the public have an interest, where a trivial sum or matter is in dispute, or where a reasonable offer in settlement has been turned down.[13]

There have been several judicial review decisions both on the 'reasonableness' test for granting applications and other discretionary powers of the Board, from which it appears that the Court of Session is reluctant to interfere with the exercise of the Board's discretion. Perhaps the best example is *McTear v Scottish Legal Aid Board*.[14] The petitioner had applied for legal aid for an action for reparation against a tobacco company, based on the allegation that her husband had contracted cancer and died as a result of smoking the company's cigarettes.

---
[11] 1983 SLT 616.
[12] *Ibid.*, at 618.
[13] *The Law and Practice of Legal Aid in Scotland, op cit.*, at 9–21.
[14] (Unreported) 15 February 1995 (Court of Session) (opinion of Lord Kirkwood).

The petitioner had obtained an opinion from senior counsel in support of her application for legal aid, indicating that the deceased had clear *probabilis causa*, good prospects of success, and that the claim was worth about £100,000. However, legal aid was refused on the grounds that there were serious doubts as to whether the petitioner would succeed, that the case would be difficult, complex, lengthy and expensive, and that it would not be reasonable to hazard a large sum of public money on a case with such limited prospects of success. The court considered that the Board's decision to refuse legal aid was not *Wednesbury*[15] unreasonable. *McTear* also confirms that the likely cost of litigation could be the dominant factor in the decision to refuse legal aid, although it could never be the sole consideration.

All of the reported cases to date in which petitioners have sought judicial review of decisions of the Board have arisen from the refusal of, or other decisions taken in relation to, legal aid applications which were not, themselves, for judicial review, for example reparation cases. None have arisen from situations in which the original legal aid application was to pursue a judicial review against a body other than the Board, for example a local authority. At the time of writing, therefore, there is no formal differentiation between applications to fund judicial reviews and the general run of civil legal aid applications either in legislation, judicial interpretation, or the Board's guidance.[16]

In practice, applications for legal aid for judicial review are handled slightly differently from other civil legal aid applications. All applications for civil legal aid must be made on the Board's standard form. The application form includes a financial statement and a statement by the applicant which should explain the nature of the client's case and the precise matters for which legal aid is required. This statement is intimated to the opponent named in the application, who is entitled to object to the grant of legal aid. The application should be accompanied, so far as possible, by such precognitions and other documents as the Board may need to determine the application. In a judicial review legal aid application, it would be good practice for the statement to specify precisely the decision or action complained of, including relevant dates, refer to the legislation under which the decision or action was taken, explain which of the grounds of judicial review is being relied upon, and why the decision or action is defective in terms of those grounds. It would also be good practice for the application to be accompanied by a copy of the decision complained of (if available) and, in most cases, the client's precognition.

The application, once received, is notified to the opponent. It then proceeds to scrutiny of means and merits. Both stages of scrutiny are the responsibility of the Board staff. However, scrutiny of the papers on the merits may be carried out by an external reporter rather than a permanent employee of the Board. Such reporters may be solicitors, or junior or senior counsel. The majority of

---

[15] *Associated Provincial Picture Houses Ltd v Wednesbury Corporation* [1948] 1 KB 223.
[16] This comment applies to the generality of applications for legal aid for the purpose of judicial review. Where the application is for legal aid to review a decision of the Board, s 14(4) requires a different procedure, which is discussed below.

applications in judicial review matters are considered by external reporters who are regarded as particularly qualified in the subject-matter of judicial review. Difficult or controversial applications may be discussed by the Board's Legal Services Group and may go to a subcommittee for decision.

The general trend is increasingly towards carrying out scrutiny of merits in-house, but judicial review cases appear to form an exception to the general approach in that only a few applications are considered in-house, and they are usually sent to external reporters. In judicial review cases, the reporters are almost exclusively advocates, and, in many cases, senior counsel. If the reporter considers that legal aid will be granted that will normally be confirmed and the decision to award legal aid intimated to the applicant. Where the reporter's view is that legal aid should not be granted, that view will also normally be confirmed. The reporter's views are monitored by a member of the Board's staff for conformity with existing Board policy, who would then formulate the reasons for refusal (if appropriate) and communicate them to the applicant. There is no direct communication between external reporters and applicants.

For a number of years, the reasons given for refusal were brief and only indicated which of the statutory grounds formed the basis for refusal. Since early 1994, the practice has changed and fuller reasons are given which are specific to the particular case. However, the indication of reasons is still very brief.

If an application is refused, the applicant has a right to have the decision reviewed by the Board.[17] An application for review must be made on the standard form and lodged with the Board within 15 days of notice of refusal being given. An application may be lodged late where there is special reason, and, in practice, late applications are permitted when accompanied by appropriate reasons for lateness. The application for review should be intimated to the opponent. The regulations make no further provision for the conduct of the review. The review is internal to the Board.

The procedure followed within the Board for conducting reviews has recently changed. Formerly, the case papers were sent to two people, one in-house, and one external reporter. If they agreed, a decision to that effect would normally have been confirmed; if they disagreed, the papers were sent to a third person for consideration. A decision on review would then have been issued based on the majority opinion. If the reasons for refusal on review were to be different from the reasons given for the original decision, the Board's policy was to give the applicant's solicitor an opportunity to comment on the new reasons.

Under the revised procedure the application for review is now first sent to a single in-house solicitor who is empowered to admit the application. If that person recommends refusal, the application must then be sent to an external reporter. If the reporter agrees with the recommendation to refuse, that determines the outcome of the application. If, instead, the external reporter recommends that the application be admitted in whole or in part, it is referred to a second in-house solicitor, and the majority view determines the outcome.

---

[17] 1986 Avc, section 14(3), and Civil Legal Aid (Scotland) Regulations 1987, (SI 1987 No 381), reg 20.

5 LEGAL AID AND JUDICIAL REVIEW

The only further recourse for an applicant dissatisfied by a review decision is judicial review in the Court of Session. An applicant seeking judicial review of an adverse decision on the award of legal aid will usually wish to apply for legal aid to fund the judicial review. If the Board were to determine such an application solely through its normal procedure, there would be an obvious concern over the impartiality of the review process. The Act, therefore, provides for a special review procedure[18] whereby if an application for legal aid to fund an action against the Board is refused, and the applicant asks for a review, the Board, unless it decides to grant the application forthwith, must refer the application and supporting documents 'to the sheriff for Lothian and Borders at Edinburgh'. This form of wording is interpreted as meaning any of the sheriffs at Edinburgh. The sheriff has complete authority to decide the issues of *probabilis causa* and reasonableness, and the Board must make legal aid available if he so decides. The papers may include the Board's observations on the application. Such observations will include a response to any arguments made by the applicant in his application for review. In practice, the papers are sent to the sheriff clerk who allocates the case to one of the sheriffs for decision. There is apparently no attempt to channel applications under this procedure to particular sheriffs, and they appear to be allocated on the basis of sheriffs' availability.

The special review procedure comes into play only once the application has been refused. The Board is still legally responsible for the initial decision on the application for judicial review of its prior decision. However, internal procedures are different from those for routine applications. These too have recently been changed. Initially, the papers, including those relating to the decision on the prior application whose refusal gave rise to the application for legal aid for judicial review, will be looked at briefly by an official of the Board. That official will consider whether there is any obvious fault with the consideration of the first application which might easily be remedied. If not, a paper is prepared for the Legal Services subcommittee (formerly the Legal Aid subcommittee). At this stage, consideration of the first application may be reopened and the applicant's solicitor invited to comment on relevant matters. The subcommittee will consider the matter. Formerly, the subcommittee merely recommended a disposal, but now it decides itself on behalf of the Board and will intimate the decision to the applicant. If the decision is favourable, that disposes of the review; if the decision is unfavourable, the applicant may ask for it to be given further consideration. If he does so, the matter will be referrred to the Legal Services Committee, which will make a further decision. If that decision is favourable to the applicant, it can be intimated immediately. In the past, an unfavourable decision might have been further considered by the full Board, but this no longer happens.

If, once the process described above is complete, the final decision is a refusal, the applicant has the right of review, and the special procedure under section 14(4) of the Act (described above) is followed. It should be clear from

---

[18] Section 14(4).

this account that where the Board adheres to its original decision, and the case is then referred to the sheriff, there is considerable potential for delay. However, this potential for delay should have been reduced by the recent simplification of internal procedures.

Number and distribution of legal aid applications

Table 1 gives an indication of the number and subject-matter of applications for legal aid for judicial review received in the financial years 1992/93 and 1993/94. These tables are based on the tables supplied by the Board. Both the numbers and percentages require to be treated with some caution. The total number of applications shown for each year is correct; however, the number and percentage of applications in each subject category are not the actual figures, but estimated, as there were some difficulties in identifying the subject-matter of some applications for legal aid. All applications for legal aid are recorded in the Board's computer system; however, this contains very limited information. The Board's staff derived the information as to subject-matter supplied to us from manual records. A significant proportion of the manual records for judicial review cases were not available[19] and, as a result, the subject-matter of these cases could not be identified. In making up the tables for the two years, the Board staff assumed that the breakdown of subject-matter in the 'missing files' was the same as in those for which the manual records were available. This, of course, is a questionable assumption. The true figures would probably have been different if all the manual records had been available, and it is difficult to estimate how different. The figures must, therefore, be treated as only broadly indicative of the breakdown by subject-matter of legal aid applications for judicial review, and their reliability as indicators is clearly at its most limited with regard to the numerically small categories.

In 1992/93, 176 applications were received, rising to 222 in 1993/94.[20] The largest categories in both years were housing cases (32.9% in 1992/93 and 38.7% in 1993/94) and immigration control cases (27.3% in 1992/93 and 15.3% in 1993/94). The housing cases are dominated by homelessness cases, which were 30.1% of all applications in 1992/93, and 29.7% in 1993/94. The only other large categories of cases were applications for legal aid for judicial review of Scottish Legal Aid Board decisions, of criminal injuries compensation decisions, and social security cases. Applications for judicial review of Board decisions accounted for 9.7% of applications in 1992/93, and 11.7% in 1993/94. Most of these were cases in which the initial application for legal aid was in a non-judicial review matter. This is one category for which we do have

---
[19] For 1992/93, manual records were available for 140 of the 176 cases (79.6%). For 1993/94, manual records were available for 188 of 222 cases (84.7%).
[20] The rise in numbers continued in 1994/95, with 237 applications being lodged in that year.

Table 5.1 Number and subject-matter of applications for legal aid for judicial review

Subject	Applications received 1992/93 No	% of total	Applications Received 1993/94 No	% of total	Total No
Homeless persons	53	30.1%	66	29.7%	119
Other housing cases	5	2.8%	20	9.0%	25
Education legislation	6	3.4%	4	1.8%	10
Town and country planning	0	0.0%	4	1.8%	4
Compulsory purchase	0	0.0%	0	0.0%	0
Licensing	1	0.6%	1	0.5%	2
Mental health legislation	3	1.7%	2	0.9%	5
Other social welfare law	4	2.3%	2	0.9%	6
Local government (other)	4	2.3%	0	0.0%	4
Social security	15	8.5%	23	10.4%	38
Immigration control	48	27.3%	34	15.3%	82
Prisoners rights	3	1.7%	6	2.7%	9
Public sector employment	0	0.0%	0	0.0%	0
Criminal injuries compensation	9	5.1%	12	5.4%	21
Legal aid	17	9.7%	26	11.7%	43
Other	8	4.5%	22	9.9%	30
Totals	176	100%	222	100%	398

the 1994/95 figure which, at 25, is 10.5% of all applications. Social security matters provided 8.5% of applications in 1992/93 and 10.4% in 1993/94.[21] Applications for review of decisions of the Criminal Injuries Compensation Board were 5.1 % of cases in 1992/93, and 5.4% in 1993/94. The 'other' category represents all cases not falling within the scheme of subject-classification supplied by us to the Board, and accounted for 4.5% of applications in 1992/93, rising to 9.9% in 1993/94.

The distribution of subject-matter of legal aid applications may be compared to that for petitions for judicial review. We were not able to match up legal aid applications with petitions for judicial review, by tracing the progress of cases from legal aid applications to petitions lodged in court. However, it would seem reasonable to compare the figures for legal aid applications for judicial review for the financial years 1992/93 and 1993/94, with the court statistics for the calendar years 1992 and 1993.

The major reason for comparing the court statistics with those for legal aid applications is to get a better idea of the level of demand for judicial review, as there may be a substantial demand for legal action to challenge decisions of public authorities which is not being translated into court statistics. In those areas dominated by commercial interests, there are no formal obstacles to surmount before petitioning for judicial review. However, for clients on low incomes who inevitably dominate categories such as housing, social security and prisoners' rights, the requirement to obtain legal aid is an important hurdle.

---

[21] Housing benefit cases are included as social security rather than housing.

There are marked differences between the two sets of figures. Some categories which figure prominently in the court statistics are much less prominent in the legal aid statistics. However, the explanation is generally that cases in these categories tend to be brought by commercial clients who can normally afford to pay for representation themselves. The 'commercial law' areas, which provide the largest numbers of cases in the court statistics, are licensing and town and country planning. Licensing provided 11 cases in 1992 (9.4% of the total) and 25 in 1993 (16.6%),[22] but only two legal aid applications in 1992–94 were concerned with licensing representing, less than 1% of all legal aid applications. The contrast with regard to planning and land use is less profound. They provided eight cases in 1992 (6.8%) and five cases in 1993 (3.3%), no legal aid applications in 1992/93 and four legal aid applications in 1993/94. Although the ratio of legal aid applications to judicial review petitions is much higher with planning than with respect to licensing, the number of legal aid applications is small and, all applications occurred in one year, which may have been atypical. No firm conclusions can be drawn, therefore, from this difference.

The second largest category in the court statistics is housing cases. There were 26 of these in 1992 (22% of the total) of which 22 (85%) were homelessness. In practice, homeless petitioners are almost always legally aided. There were, again, 26 housing cases in 1993 (only 17% of the total) of which, again, 22 (85%) were homelessness. By contrast, in 1992/93, there were 53 applications for legal aid relating to homelessness, and five relating to other housing matters. In 1993/94 there were 66 applications relating to homelessness, and 20 relating to other housing matters.[23] Therefore, it appears that roughly two-and-a-half to three times as many persons are applying for legal aid to challenge homelessness decisions as are lodging petitions in court.

A similar contrast appears with social security benefits. There were three such petitions in 1992, and six in 1993, but 15 applications for legal aid in 1992/93, and 22 in 1993/94. Applications in the two financial years for prisoners' rights cases were three and six, which compare to none and one petition in court.

The largest category in the court statistics is immigration, with 36 and 55 cases in 1992 and 1993 respectively. Here, there is an approximate equivalence of legal aid applications and judicial reviews, with 48 of the former in 1992/93 and 34 in 1993/94. However, in a large proportion of immigration control cases, the petitioner is not legally aided.[24] As immigration control is an area in which a substantial proportion of the petitioners are able to pay their own legal fees, it makes more sense to compare the number of legal aid applications with the number of petitions in which the petitioner was legally aided. If we do that, we find that 10 of the 36 immigration petitions in 1992 were legally aided (in

---

[22] See Table 2 in Chapter 3, at p 19.
[23] As indicated above, these figures are estimates rather than actual figures, as are all the figures for particular subject-matters.
[24] See Table 5 in Chapter 4. Only 37.8 % of petitioners in immigration cases have legal aid, according to court records. This probably understates the true position slightly.

5 LEGAL AID AND JUDICIAL REVIEW

one further case the petitioner may have had legal aid).[25] In 1993, 15 of the 55 petitions were definitely legally aided, and in a further five cases legal aid may have been granted. It appears that there are approximately three times as many applications for legal aid in immigration matters as there are petitions. However, all that these comparisons tell us is that there are many more people who consult a solicitor about legal action in the broad field of welfare law, than ultimately seek judicial review of administrative decisions by lodging a petition in court. They cannot tell us the reasons for the gap. The likely reasons for the gap are, first, that in some cases where legal aid is granted the respondent settles before the matter gets to court and, secondly, that many legal aid applications are not granted. It can probably be assumed that nearly all applicants who are refused legal aid do not proceed to lodge a petition. This raises the issue of the rate at which legal aid applications are granted, which we discuss below.[26]

Table 2 gives an indication of the geographical distribution of legal aid applications for judicial review. The table shows the number of outlets seeking legal aid for judicial review according to the town in which the outlet is located. It can be assumed that no such applications were received from towns not listed in the table. The term 'outlet' refers to an *office* of a firm rather than a firm or a particular solicitor. Table 2 also shows the total number of legal aid applications received from outlets in the towns in question.

Our analysis of the geographical origins of the judicial review caseload revealed a somewhat uneven distribution.[27] However, the overall distribution masks greater unevenness within particular categories such as homelessness and social security. Given the unevenness of the judicial review caseload in welfare law matters, it is not surprising to find a markedly uneven geographical distribution of legal aid applications. As Table 2 shows, Dundee (Scotland's fourth largest city, with 3.4% of the population (171,520[28])) could muster only three applications in two years, less than 1% of the total number of applications received by the Board. In comparison, Stranraer, the principal town of Wigtown District Council with, at 30,077, less than one-sixth of Dundee's population, accounted for 14 applications in two years (3.5% of the total received by the Board). Paisley, the principal town of Renfrew District Council, with a population only slightly greater than Dundee's, at 201,000, mustered 19 applications in two years (4.8% of total applications). Glasgow accounted for 148 applications (37.2% of the total), despite having only 13.3% of the Scottish population. East Kilbride, with a population of 82,777, accounted for only one application, and a number of substantial population centres do not figure at all, including

---

[25] In theory, the case papers should always indicate the fact where a person has legal aid; however, in practice this is not always done.
[26] See Table 3 and associated text.
[27] See Table 5 of Chapter 3, at pp 26, 27.
[28] Population figures are latest estimates from *Whittaker's Almanac 1995*. As the four cities are all district councils, the population figures are, by definition, the number of persons in the area of that district council. In the case of the smaller towns referred to in the body of the text, we have given the population figures for the local authority areas in which they are situated. It can be assumed that no legal aid applications were received from other towns in those areas.

Table 5.2 Geographical distribution of legal aid applications for judicial review

	1992–93		1993–94		
Location of outlets	No of outlets seeking legal aid for JR	No of applications received for JR	No of outlets seeking legal aid for JR	No of applications received for JR	Total applications
Aberdeen	1	2	3	13	15
Aidrie	2	2	2	4	6
Alloa	1	1	1	1	2
Ayr	4	7	6	12	19
Baillieston	1	1	0	0	1
Barrhead	0	0	1	1	1
Bathgate	1	2	0	0	2
Bellshill	1	1	2	3	4
Brechin	0	0	1	1	1
Clydebank	1	1	0	0	1
Coatbridge	1	1	1	1	2
Cumbernauld	0	0	2	4	4
Cupar	1	1	0	0	1
Dalkeith	2	3	0	0	3
Drumchapel	1	1	0	0	1
Dumfries	1	1	0	0	1
Dundee	2	2	1	1	3
Dunfermline	3	6	2	4	10
Dunoon	0	0	1	1	1
East Kilbride	1	1	0	0	1
Edinburgh	18	37	13	40	77
Falkirk	0	0	1	1	1
Forres	1	1	0	0	1
Fort William	1	5	1	1	6
Glasgow	19	67	27	88	155
Inverness	1	1	2	2	3
Irvine	1	1	0	0	1
Kilsyth	1	1	1	1	2
Kirkcaldy	2	4	3	6	10
Leven	0	0	1	1	1
Livingston	0	0	1	4	4
Motherwell	2	2	0	0	2
Musselburgh	0	0	1	1	1
Paisley	4	8	3	11	19
Perth	1	1	2	2	3
Saltcoats	0	0	1	1	1
Stirling	1	1	1	4	5
Stranraer	2	6	2	8	14
Uddingston	0	0	1	1	1
Whitburn	0	0	1	2	2
Wishaw	2	8	1	2	10
Totals	80	176	85	222	398

Greenock, Kilmarnock and Hamilton. We recognise that the place of origin of the grievance is not necessarily the same as the location of the solicitor's office which makes the legal aid application. However, clients in the welfare law areas will normally consult a local solicitor. The figures do, therefore, appear to warrant the general conclusion that there is a markedly uneven geographical distribution of legal aid applications.

There appear to have been no applications from any outlets in Borders Region, although it has a population of 105,300 (2.1% of the Scottish total), whereas an even distribution according to population would have resulted in eight over two years. By contrast, Nithsdale District Council, in neighbouring Dumfries and Galloway Region, with a population of only 57,220 (1.1% of the Scottish total) accounts for 12 applications. Aberdeen is a particularly interesting case, with applications jumping from two to 13 in successive years. From the court statistics and other information available, it is clear that it is the 1992/93 figures, rather than the 1993/94 figures, which are similar to earlier years. The main reason for the increase appears to have been that homelessness applications relating to Aberdeen and some nearby towns appear to have taken off in 1993,[29] although other types of case also figure, whereas, in the period from the introduction of the specialised procedure in 1985 up to 1993, there was very little apparent demand for judicial review in the field of welfare law in the Aberdeen area.

One would not expect legal aid applications to be evenly distributed according to population, as the factors which are likely to generate a demand for judicial review, and, hence, influence the number of applications, do not apply to the same degree in all areas. In the case of immigration control, the largest category of application, it is likely that the distribution of ethnic minority populations is a major factor, and this distribution is uneven. In the case of housing, the second largest of the welfare categories, the relevant factors are likely to include the proportion of local authority-owned housing stock, and the relative pressure of demand for social-rented housing stock, which is itself a compound of more specific variables. Given that housing is a local authority function, and that local authorities have significant discretion, both with regard to homelessness and allocation of council housing in general, one might also expect variation in local authority policies to have an impact. There might also be differences as between local authorities in the general quality and efficiency of housing administration which would have implications for the number of potentially reviewable decisions. We would, therefore, expect some discrepancy between population distribution and the demand for judicial review in the housing field.

However, the geographical variations in the incidence of housing cases are extremely large, and the particular distribution we have found cannot, in fact, be plausibly explained by the likely differentiating factors, including those

---

[29] The majority of the legal aid applications in question are submitted by a single solicitor. They relate to cases against Aberdeen District Council and other neighbouring councils.

described above. Thus, there appears to be no clear split between predominantly urban and predominantly rural areas; nor is the number of applications closely correlated to the degree of pressure on housing stock and the socio-economic profile of the population. We did not undertake a systematic study of variations in policy, or the quality of administration across local authorities – only two local authorities were studied in depth.[30] However, the impact studies enabled us to determine the reasons for comparatively frequent resort to judicial review against two housing authorities. In addition, the adviser survey provided much useful information about a number of other local authorities, their policies, and the quality of their adminstration. These different sources of information point to the conclusion that the uneven geographical distribution of legal aid applications is, indeed, significant. It appears that the pattern of submission of legal aid applications is only partly determined by the objective needs[31] of particular local populations for facilities for challenging public authority decisions. As the next chapter will illustrate, other factors have had a major influence.

The figures for the geographical distribution also give us some idea of the involvement of solicitors generally in judicial review. In 1992/93, the Board received applications for legal aid for judicial review from 80 outlets out of 1266 eligible to apply for legal aid, and the 1029 which, in fact, submitted at least one civil legal application in that year. In 1993/94, judicial review legal aid applications were received from 85 outlets out of 1302 eligible to apply, and the 1002 making at least one civil legal aid application in that year. It appears, therefore, that in each year solicitors in between 6% and 7% of legal aid outlets applied for legal aid for judicial review. Thus, although judicial review is clearly a minority pursuit, it is one carried on by a significant proportion of Scottish solicitors.

However, as far as we can determine, applications for legal aid are not evenly spread across those solicitors who are making applications. In 1992/93, 176 applications were submitted from 80 outlets, an average of just over two per outlet. In 1993/94, 222 applications were submitted by 85 outlets, an average of a little more than two-and-a-half applications per outlet. This suggests that the average solicitor involved in judicial review has only a small caseload. However, it is relevant to look at the actual distribution of applications across solicitors, as well as the average number. We were not able to obtain an exhaustive breakdown of which solicitors applied for legal aid for judicial review, and how many applications they made in general, but the Board was able to provide a breakdown of those applications which could be clearly identified as housing cases (the largest category), and this is of some assistance in seeing how applications are spread across solicitors. In 1992–94 there was a total of 104 housing-related applications from 35 firms, giving an average of three applications per

---

[30] See Chapter 7.
[31] We are assuming that where a person has an arguable case that a public authority has acted unlawfully there is a need for legal advice and representation. For a discussion of the theoretical difficulties involved in making assumptions about the existence of legal need, see P Morris, R White, and R Lewis, *Social Needs and Legal Action* (Martin Robertson, 1973), especially pp 73–87.

firm.[32] In fact, the average figure is likely to be less than that, as some applications are submitted by Edinburgh agents on behalf of local agents, and Edinburgh agents had, in some cases, submitted applications from more than one local agent. Few firms are close to the average. One law centre submitted 10 applications; one private firm (an Edinburgh agent) submitted 11 applications; and a third (a local agent) submitted 10 applications. One firm submitted six applications, four submitted five applications each, and three submitted four applications each. Two firms submitted three applications each, six firms submitted two applications each and 16 firms submitted one application each. Amalgamating these figures, across Scotland only 15 firms submitted more than two applications relating to housing matters in a 24-month period.[33] The reasons for these apparent concentrations of specialism are likely to have something to do with the local housing environment, including local authority policies. However, as the conclusion above implies, we do not think that the concentration of casework amongst a small number of solicitors merely reflects a variation in local needs for legal advice and representation. We think that it also reflects the fact that a limited number of firms take an active interest in, and have expertise in, housing matters whatever the local housing environment. In addition, as we shall see when we consider the results of the adviser survey and the impact study, a major factor determining whether solicitors get involved in judicial review is the operation of the system of referral from lay advice agencies.

We do not have equivalent information relating to other subject specialisms within judicial review. However, the evidence from our adviser survey[34] suggests that in other areas, particularly immigration, legal aid applications are strongly clustered rather than being evenly distributed amongst solicitors.

Reverting to housing, the information we have suggests that the remedy of judicial review is being underexploited in the housing field, despite its forming the largest category of legal aid application. However, the low numbers in certain other categories, notably prisoners' rights cases and social security cases, suggest that judicial review may also be being underused in those categories. Here, comparisons with England and Wales may be helpful. We have already seen that there is a higher ratio of judicial reviews per head of population in England. This is also reflected in the legal aid statistics provided by similar research in England and Wales.[35] There is a higher rate of application overall, and higher rates of application in some of the particular areas under discussion.

---

[32] The figure of 104 represents cases clearly identified from records as housing cases. If the subject distribution of applications in which the subject-matter could clearly be identified holds good for *all* applications in 1992–94, there would have been a further 40 housing-related applications over two years. Thus, both the total number of firms, and the number of applications for some firms, are likely to have been higher than indicated here.
[33] As the point made in the preceding note applies equally here, there may, in fact, have been more firms which submitted more than two housing-related applications.
[34] See Chapter 6.
[35] M Sunkin, L Bridges and G Mészáros, *Judicial Review in Perspective* 2nd ed (Cavendish, 1996). The legal aid research is to be found in Chapter 4.

In the quarter studied, the English researchers found 27 applications relating to prisoners' rights. If the quarter was representative, that would equate to 104 applications in a year. In Scotland, the number of prisoners' rights applications in 1992/93 was only three, although there was a 100% increase to six in 1993/94. If Scotland produced the same number of applications per head of population, it would produce approximately 10 per year. Perhaps not very much can be made of the comparison as we do not know which of the two years is more representative of the general pattern, and only a few more cases on the 1993/94 figure would produce equivalence. However, quite apart from any comparison, the figures for Scotland seem low in absolute terms. It seems improbable that Scotland is capable of producing only nine such applications in two years. However, these numbers are low, so the problem of the missing files assumes larger proportions, and the reliability of 'grossing up' figures declines. The conclusion of underuse in this area must, therefore, be treated with considerable caution.

Comparing social security-related applications is more complicated. In our research the social security category includes housing benefit, whereas in the English research it is classified as 'other housing'. However, the quarter studied cannot be considered representative for housing benefit, as it included 121 housing benefit cases, almost all derived from a single solicitor in Liverpool. It is, therefore, more appropriate to compare all other benefit cases for the two jurisdictions. In England and Wales there were 20 such cases in the quarter studied, suggesting a figure of approximately 80 for the whole of 1991. For Scotland, the figures for 1992/93 and 1993/94 (excluding housing benefit) are 11 and 15 applications respectively, which suggests that Scotland produces roughly one-and-a-half times as many social security cases per head of population as England and Wales. However, although there does not seem to be a dearth of social security cases in comparison to England and Wales, in absolute terms these figures seem a little low. It is true that the social security area is one in which there are statutory rights of appeal which are extensively used. However, there are two important areas where no right of appeal to an independent judicial tribunal exists, namely housing benefit and the social fund. There are also opportunities for judicial review in relation to those benefits (the majority) for which rights of appeal do exist. Even in relation to these benefits, there are some matters which may not be appealed, for example delay in making decisions, and 'interlocutory' decisions taken in the appellate process, such as the grant and refusal of leave to appeal, and the setting aside of tribunal decisions. Given the enormous volume of decisions taken by the Benefits Agency and concerns about the quality of social security benefit decision-making,[36] one would expect more activity in this area.

---

[36] See, for example, R Sainsbury, 'The Social Security Chief Adjudication Officer' 1989 *Public Law* 323. The article is based on Annual Reports of the Chief Adjudication Officer. Subsequent annual reports suggest that the weaknesses in decision-making reviewed in Sainsbury's article continue to be a problem. Concerns about quality of decision-making also emerge from research into housing benefit, and annual and special reports of the Parliamentary Commisioner for Adminstration.

Thus, it appears that despite the prominence of some welfare law topics in the court and legal aid statistics, judicial review continues to be underused in the welfare law area. This apparent underuse of judicial review is not surprising, as there has been concern for years that there is an unmet legal need in these areas, and the most recent research tends to confirm this. Paterson and Turner-Kerr's comprehensive research for the Scottish Legal Aid Board into the supply and distribution of legal aid in Scotland[37] found that the provision of advice and assistance (a broader measure of those seeking assistance from solicitors than civil legal aid applications) in aspects of social welfare law was sporadically distributed across Scotland, and that the level of provision is low in absolute terms.

Our findings on the distribution of legal aid applications mirror those of the research undertaken in England and Wales. Both the distribution of legal aid applications for judicial review in general and for particular subject areas were heavily skewed towards particular geographical areas rather than being distributed in proportion to population. Homelessness and immigration control legal aid applications, the two most numerous categories, were very heavily concentrated in the London area. There were also pronounced clusters of education and mental health applications in certain areas, which appeared to be due to the location of the small number of solicitors specialising in these subjects.[38]

Speed of processing applications

In 1992/93 the average time taken to process a legal aid application was seven weeks, falling to six weeks in 1993/94 despite a 26% increase in the number of applications from 176 to 222. In 1992/93, 52% of applications were processed in six weeks or less, 26% in six–eight weeks, and 22% in eight weeks or more. For 1993/94, the corresponding figures are 57%, 18% and 25% respectively. Overall, these figures appear to be satisfactory and, for the general run of litigants, do not add a great deal of delay to that which arises from other stages of the legal process. In fact, they indicate that, on average, applications relating to judicial review are processed slightly more slowly than the generality of civil legal aid applications.[39] The Board managed to turn round 81% of such applications in less than six weeks in 1992/93, and 76% in less than six weeks in 1993/94. Only 12% of all civil applications in 1992/93 and only 10% in 1993/94 took more than eight weeks to process, compared to 22% and 25% in those years for judicial review applications. Before submitting a civil legal aid application, the client may have been advised under the legal advice and assistance scheme. It is unlikely, however, that additional delay could arise at this stage, since the solicitor,

---

[37] A Paterson, M Turner-Kerr, *Research Report on the Distribution of the Supply of Legal Aid in Scotland* (Scottish Legal Aid Board, 1994).
[38] See *Judicial Review in Perspective, op. cit.*
[39] The reasons for this are not clear, but part of the explanation may be that many applications are initially granted under the urgency provisions, and the papers required for the full application are not always forwarded timeously.

in effect, grants advice and assistance himself. There should be no delay in securing funding for pre-litigation advice and assistance unless the solicitor wishes to exceed the normal limits of expenditure.

However, even the periods of time quoted above might appear to be unacceptable delays to a large proportion of applicants for legal aid for judicial review whose problems require urgent resolution. These would include many homeless applicants and some immigration applicants, for example those alleging unlawful detention and those facing deportation. Applications relating to the homelessness legislation accounted for 31% (122 in all) of all applications over the two-year period. Applications relating to immigration control accounted for 21% (82 in all).

There were 95 applications under the special urgency provisions[40] in 1992/93, and 100 in 1993/94. There are two types of urgency application. Under the first, a solicitor seeks *retrospective* authority for a specific step taken to protect the applicant's position (reg 18(1)(a) notification),[41] such as entering appearance. The second type is the usual type of urgency application and requires the prior approval of the Board before any work is undertaken (reg 18(1)(b) application).[42] There were six regulation 18(1)(a) notifications in 1992/93, and four in 1993/94. It is probably better to exclude these from the analysis. If an urgent application is to be granted, there is no reason why there should be any significant delay, because the Board is willing to approve such applications provisionally by telephone. Where an application is granted on the basis of urgency, it must be followed by a full legal aid application. Fifty-two of the 89 urgent applications (reg 18(1)(b)) in 1992/93, and 63 of the 96 urgent applications in 1993/94, were granted urgency cover. The rates of granting were, therefore, 58.4% in 1992/93, and 65.6% in 1993/94. However, the rate at which applications in judicial review cases are granted is slightly higher than that for urgency applications generally. In 1992/93 there were 4249 regulation 18(1)(b) applications, of which 2267 were granted (53.4%). In 1993/94 there were 4228 applications, of which 2416 were granted (57.1%).

Some solicitors reported difficulties in persuading the Board that the urgency provisions should be applied in some homelessness cases. On the face of it, this seems odd, although there will be circumstances in which there is arguably no urgency, for example where the applicant has satisfactory temporary accommodation, and some urgent applications in homelessness cases are refused for precisely this reason. We are not able to ask the reasons for such refusals or how frequently this arises because of the confidentiality of the Board's files. Other solicitors claimed to obtain emergency legal aid in homelessness cases without difficulty, and the Board has stated that, where the applicants are 'passported' through the legal aid means test because they are dependant on the appropriate social security benefits (as most homeless applicants are), it is possible to turn round a full legal aid application in 14 days.

---

[40] Civil Legal Aid (Scotland) Regulations 1987, reg 18.
[41] *Ibid.*, reg 18(1)(a).
[42] *Ibid.*, reg 18(1)(b).

Where an application is refused, but subsequently granted on review, there is inevitably an additional delay before litigation can commence. We have already noted the potential for delay in the review process, and some solicitors and advisers interviewed for the third element of our research referred to cases which had gone to review where, in their view, the supposed speed of judicial review itself as a remedy had been undermined by the delays occasioned by the overall time taken to obtain legal aid.

Grant and refusal of legal aid applications

The most interesting and relevant questions arising from a study of the legal aid hurdle relate to the fairness of decision-making, in particular whether decisions to grant or refuse legal aid are appropriate, in the sense that the statutory criteria are correctly and reasonably applied. If decision-making were too strict and meritorious applications were refused, the legal aid system would be acting as an improper barrier to the redress of citizens' grievances against the administration. If decision-making were lax and allowed groundless applications through, then public authorities would be being subjected to an unnecessary burden of frequently defending perfectly lawful and reasonable actions in the courts. As we shall see in Chapter 6, the fairness of the Board's decision-making is a matter of considerable concern to solicitors working in the area of administrative law.

Statistics on rates of granting and refusing legal aid cannot, of course, tell us whether legal aid decision-making is fair and reasonable, but they may shed some light on the question. Table 3 shows the number of applications submitted and the number and proportion granted, refused or abandoned. The table is derived from the results of initial applications, and the 'granted' column does not include applications granted after review.

In 1992/93, 23.3% of applications (41) were initially granted, 66.5% (117) were initially refused, and 10.2% (18) were abandoned. If abandonments are excluded, the initial grant rate becomes 25.9% and the refusal rate 74.1%. In 47 cases, the solicitor applied for a review of a refusal, and 17 of these applications

Table 5.3 Rates of grant and refusal of applications for legal aid for judicial review

	1992/93		1993/94		Total 1992–94	
	No	%	No	%	No	%
Received	176	100%	222	100%	398	100%
Granted initially	41	23.3%	68	30.6%	109	27.4%
Granted on review	17	9.7%	16	7.2%	33	14.9%
Total grants	58	33%	84	37.8%	142	35.7%
Refused	100	56.8%	125	56.3%	225	56.5%
Abandoned	18	10.2%	13	5.9%	31	7.8%

were granted after review, pushing the overall success rate (excluding abandonments) to 36.7% (58). In 1993/94, 30.6% of applications (68) were granted initially, 63.5% were refused (141), and 5.9% were abandoned (13). If abandonments are excluded, the grant rate becomes 32.5% and the refusal rate 67.5%. In 64 cases the solicitor applied for a review of a refusal, and 16 of these applications were granted after review, pushing the overall success rate for 1993/94 to 40.2% (84) (excluding abandonments). Thus, there is a sizeable difference in success rates on initial application as between the two years, which narrows once reviews are added in. Aggregating the figures for the two years, it appears that, excluding abandonments, less than one-third of applications (29.7%) are granted initially, and less than two-fifths (38.7%) are granted once successful reviews are added in.

It is instructive to compare these figures both with the rate of success in civil legal applications generally in Scotland, and with those found in the study of legal aid applications for judicial review in England and Wales.[43] The annual reports of the Board do not disclose success rates directly. What they show is the number of applications received and the number of grants in each year. Since some applications will be disposed of in a different year from that in which they are considered, the figure for applications includes some cases whose disposal will have occurred during the following year, and the figure for grants will include some cases which are not included in the applications figure for that year. A comparison of the two figures for a given year gives a rough guide to success rates rather than an exact picture. If we make such a comparison for Scotland, then the figure for grants expressed as a percentage of the figure for applications received in the period 1989/90 to 1993/94 varied between 69.3% and 76.3%,[44] although the rate at which applications are granted for Court of Session actions appears to be noticeably lower than for sheriff court actions.[45] It is also worth noting that there is considerable variation in success rates according to the category of application. Grant rates for the various kinds of matrimonial applications tend to be markedly higher than average. If we look only at non-matrimonial civil legal aid[46] applications, the rate of granting as a proportion of applications in the same years varied between 41.2% and 66.5% for Court of Session applications, and between 46.8% and 71.4% for sheriff court applications. These are marked fluctuations, but taking an average across these years, it would appear that applications for legal aid for judicial review are granted far less frequently in Scotland than applications generally.

A comparison with decisions taken by the Legal Aid Board in England and Wales shows that in that jurisdiction in the period under study nearly 67.7% of judicial review legal aid applications were granted on a legal aid officer's initial

---

[43] *Judicial Review in Perspective, op cit.*
[44] See Annual Reports of the Scottish Legal Aid Board.
[45] Scrutiny of the figures suggests that this is due to low rates of granting for reparation and matrimonial cases in the Court of Session. This, in turn, is likely to be due in part to applications being deemed more suitable for the sheriff court.
[46] The research in England and Wales compares applications for the purpose of judicial review to all *non-matrimonial* civil legal aid applications.

decision. A further 6.7% were granted on appeal, making an overall success rate of 74.4%. This overall figure masks considerable regional variation. The London office, which handles the largest number of applications, allowed 81% of all applications, including those granted on appeal. Others which granted a high proportion of applications were South West (71.4 % initially, rising to 78.5% after appeal), West Midlands (71.9%, rising to 73.7%), East Midlands (83.7%) and North Wales (86.7%). Those allowing lower proportions included South East (27.3%, rising to 39.4%), North West (36.7%, rising to 43.3%) and the South Wales office (27.2%, rising to 45.5%). Accordingly, it appears that the rate at which legal aid applications for judicial review are initially granted in Scotland is less than half the average rate in England and Wales (29.7% compared to 67.7%), and is comparable only to the lowest grant rates in the 13 area offices there. The difference between rates is less after appeal/review, but still surprisingly wide (38.7% compared to 74.4%).

Unlike our research, the English research showed the rate at which applications were granted in different subject areas. Accordingly, we cannot make a direct cross-border comparison of subject areas. It is interesting to note, however, that in England and Wales, grant rates were particularly high for homelessness cases (79.5%, rising to 84.7% after appeal) and immigration control cases (74.6% and 75.4%) and particularly low for legal aid cases (40%). Social security benefit cases were peculiar in that the initial grant rate was much lower than the average at 40%, but the rate rose to fully 65% after appeal.

What, therefore, explains these dramatic differences in success rates in two broadly similar jurisdictions operating broadly similar legal aid systems? It seems unlikely that the dramatic differences between success rates in Scotland and England can be explained by particular differences in the substantive law, or the administrative environment, or other factors potentially affecting the level of need for judicial review as between the two jurisdictions. As regards the substantive law, the principles of judicial review are essentially the same in Scotland and England. Much of the substantive legislation is the same (immigration control) or to equivalent effect (homelessness), and the tests to be applied in awarding legal aid appear to be very similar.[47] Clearly, there are differences in the material environment in different areas in which administrators have to work, for example differences in the characteristics of local populations, local economies, housing markets, and so forth. These might mean that administering any particular statutory scheme, such as homelessness legislation, could be a very different proposition in the two jurisdictions notwithstanding a close similarity in the legislation. However, it seems implausible that this can provide an explanation, as contextual differences between particular areas *within* the two jurisdictions are far more marked than the average differences between them.

---

[47] Legal Aid Act 1988, s 15(2), (3). The Legal Aid Board must be satisfied that the applicant has reasonable grounds for taking, defending, or being a party to proceedings, and legal aid may be refused if it would be unreasonable to grant it.

Table 5.4 Reasons for refusal of legal aid applications

	1992/93		1993/94		Total	
	No	%	No	%	No	%
Refused	100	100%	125	100%	225	100%
No probable cause	53	53%	82	65.6%	135	60%
Unreasonable	12	12%	14	11.2%	26	11.6%
No PC and unreasonable	35	35%	29	23.2%	64	28.4%

This appears to leave us with the conclusion that the major causes of the differences are more likely to be the result of one of, or some combination of, two possibilities. The first is that Scottish decision-makers are taking a more restrictive approach to granting legal aid than English decision-makers. The second is that the overall quality of applications submitted by solicitors in Scotland is substantially poorer. If the difference lies mainly in the decision-making, this, in itself, would be worthy of comment, but we would also wish to know to what extent the difference was explained by Scottish decision-makers being stricter than is appropriate, or by English decision-makers being unduly lax as compared to an ideal standard of legal aid decision-making.

We must emphasise that it is not possible to provide a clear answer to questions about the causes of the difference without direct scrutiny of legal aid case files, and the statutory confidentiality rule prevented this. However, there is some useful evidence available from our survey of solicitors and advisers which is relevant to the inquiry.

Before discussing that, it is worth looking at the breakdown of the reasons given for refusal of legal aid applications. Table 4 gives this information in terms of the statutory reasons for refusal.[48] In 1992/93, 53% of applications refused were refused solely for lack of probable cause, 12% were refused solely because it would have been unreasonable to grant legal aid, and the remaining 35% were refused for both reasons. In 1993/94, 65.6% were refused for lack of probable cause, 11.2% on reasonableness, and 23.2% for both reasons. As indicated above, these decisions are usually made by external reporters. In the opinion of the Board officer we interviewed, in those cases where both reasons are given for refusal, the lack of probable cause is usually the dominant consideration. Amalgamating the figures above, it appears that lack of probable cause was the sole reason, or one of the reasons, for refusal in 88% of the cases in 1992/93 and 89% of the cases in 1993/94. It appears, therefore, that policy issues of the type which might trigger a reasonableness refusal play a relatively small part in screening out potential judicial, reviews, since, in nearly nine-tenths of refusals, there is felt to be a weakness in the case presented by the applicant justifying a finding of no probable cause.

---

[48] These are actual figures as the Board's computer records reasons for refusal according to the statutory categories. The figures relate to those which remain refusals after *review*.

Solicitors' views on the grant and refusal of legal aid

The third element of our research was a survey of legal and lay advisers. As part of the survey we sought advisers' views on the operation of legal aid. The detailed findings are given in Chapter 6, but they are highly relevant to the present discussion. The majority of the solicitors we interviewed were unhappy to some degree with legal aid decision-making, and some were very strongly critical. They complained that meritorious cases were refused legal aid, or that they had to expend a lot of effort convincing the Board to award legal aid in worthy cases. They suggested that there was a lack of relevant expertise amongst legal aid decision-makers in that they appeared not fully to understand the substantive principles of judicial review, and the legislation and caselaw relevant to particular statutory functions. A further complaint was that the reasons given by the Board were too brief to be helpful, and did not, even after more full reasons were given, enable solicitors to tell precisely what was wrong with their applications. The Board's view is that, although fuller reasons are now given, it is not for the Board to tell solicitors in detail what information is required to be submitted in order to satisfy the statutory tests.

The views of solicitors are consistent with the hypothesis that one of the main reasons for the difference between Scottish and English statistics is that Scottish legal aid decision-makers are either too strict or simply wrong. However, can the figures be taken at face value? Solicitors clearly have a strong personal stake in the outcome of legal aid application. As explained above, we could not have access to individual files, and did not interview any of the individual external reporters which the Board uses in judicial review cases. However, we did discuss this issue with members of the Board's staff; who were of the view that, if the grant rate was substantially lower than it might be, this was due primarily to the standard of the applications. Certain faults recurred in a large proportion of applications, including poor documentation, which was often badly reconciled, the omission of essential information, failure to focus the legal arguments to be relied upon, and failure to state why the decision was thought to be unlawful in terms of the accepted principles of judicial review. Interestingly, the English researchers found that a surprisingly high proportion of applications failed to present any clear grounds for judicial review. Nonetheless, the great majority of applications were granted. They suggest that this was due to a combination of factors – the high proportion of emergency applications, the predominance of homelessness and immigration applications facilitating the build-up of expertise by officers, and the obvious fact that vital interests were at stake in most cases. This appears to suggest that decision-makers in England may be more willing to work out themselves whether the applicant has a good case rather than relying on the applicant's solicitor to make the argument, and that in general they are more willing than decision-makers in Scotland to give the applicant the benefit of any doubt. However, this is not something that could be verified without direct scrutiny of the files. A further factor that may influence grant rates in England and Wales, and might tend to produce higher grant rates, is the possibility of granting a limited certificate, which means that legal aid may be granted initially only for the purpose of applying for leave to seek judicial review.[49]

In the course of our survey of legal advisers, we also spoke to five advocates, four of whom had substantial experience of legally aided judicial review cases. The general tenor of their comments was slightly different from those made by solicitors. They thought that, in general, the standard of legal aid decision-making was not as high as it ought to be, and that the quality of decision-making was very variable. Where the emphasis of the advocates' comments differs was in their belief that the poor quality of decision-making worked both ways. It was not simply a matter of the general approach being too strict, as some (in their view) groundless applications were granted. This view was expressed on the basis of acting for petitioners as well as respondents.

None of this proves that the quality of legal aid decision-making is defective. What we can say is that there is considerable disquiet expressed by solicitors and advocates. When one also considers that grant rates are much lower than in England and Wales, it appears that there is at least a case to answer, and a need for further inquiry. Whether the explanation for the differences lies, as solicitors suggest, primarily in the decision-making process, or whether it lies in the quality of legal aid applications submitted by solicitors, it appears that Scottish residents seeking legal aid for the purposes of judicial review are not as well served as they should be, and that access to justice for the citizen is not on an equal footing in Scotland and England.

One obvious question which affects consideration of these issues is whether the difference between Scottish and English grant rates relates only to judicial review, or whether it is a general difference between the rates at which legal aid is granted in civil matters in the two jurisdictions. This appears not to be the case. In England, the national average grant rate for all non-matrimonial civil legal applications in 1991/92 was 67%, slightly lower than the grant rate for judicial review applications (75%) found in the English research. This is comparable to the figures for all civil legal aid applications in Scotland. As noted above, the figures for applications granted expressed as a proportion of applications made in Scotland in the years 1989/90–1993/94 varied between 69.3% and 76.3%. However, we also noted that for specifically non-matrimonial civil legal aid[50] applications, the rate of granting as a proportion of applications in the same years varied between 41.2% and 66.5% for Court of Session applications, and between 46.8% and 71.4% for sheriff court applications. Comparing the grant rates for all non-matrimonial cases between the two jurisdiction suggests that the rate at which applications are granted is, on the whole, lower in

---

[49] Limited certificates are discussed further below at p 81.
[50] The research in England and Wales compares applications for the purpose of judicial review to all *non-matrimonial* civil legal aid applications.

Scotland, but the difference is considerably smaller than it is for judicial review-related applications.

We have suggested that there is a concern that needs to be addressed in relation to the quality of the Board's decision-making in judicial review matters, albeit this may not be well founded. If it is not well founded that, in turn, raises questions about the general quality of solicitor's advice and casework in this area. However, to state that these matters require investigation does not close off other lines of inquiry. It may be that the differences in the rates at which legal aid is granted as between the two jurisdictions may not wholly be explained by the two factors already discussed.

The research in England and Wales found that there was a very large gap between the number of legal aid applications granted and the number of applications lodged for leave to seek judicial review.[51] The researchers suggested at least two possible explanations: one was that initial legal aid decision-making process was not as successful as it might have been at sifting out unmeritorious cases (*i.e.* decision-makers were too generous); the other was that the gap reflected a high volume of settlement of potential judicial reviews after the award of legal aid without the need for any court proceedings. The researchers were not, however, able to arrive at a definite conclusion as to the actual extent (if any) of either of these possible effects.

It appears possible that one feature of the English judicial procedure – the requirement of leave to proceed – might be having an impact here. Limited certificates are routinely granted in judicial review matters in England,[52] whereas they would not be considered in an application for judicial review in Scotland.[53] In all, 83% of English grants were limited, the limitation usually being that the legal aid certificate is used initially only for the purpose of obtaining leave to seek judicial review. It may be that the decision to grant legal aid in borderline cases tends to be tipped in favour of the applicant because of the belief that the court will knock out groundless cases at the leave stage. Whilst this phenomenon may make some contribution to the differential grant rates, the research in England and Wales does not establish that it is a major cause of high grant rates, and it is unlikely that it can be the major cause of differences in grant rates as between the two jurisdictions. Our findings for Scotland fit very well into the pattern of regional variation in England and Wales. If there were jurisdiction-wide features of the two legal aid systems which explained the differences in grant rates, one would have expected regional grant rates in England and Wales to be consistently higher than in Scotland. The fact that there are such wide regional variations in England and Wales suggests that the explanation lies more in differences in adminstrative practice as

---

[51] *Judicial Review in Perspective, op. cit.*
[52] Under s 15(4) of the Legal Aid Act 1988.
[53] There is no direct equivalent to s 15(2) of the 1988 Act. The only possibly comparable provision is s 14(2) of the Legal Aid (Scotland) Act 1986. This only allows the Board to require a person receiving civil legal aid to comply with such conditions as are expedient to enable the Board to be satisfied that it is reasonable for him to continue to receive legal aid and is not used in practice for any purpose closely resembling that of the English provision.

between legal aid offices. It is also worth stating that if the combination of the leave requirement with the practice of granting limited certificates is reducing the ability of the English system to filter out unmeritorious legal aid applications, it provides a further argument against introduction of a leave requirement in Scotland.

The outcome of legally aided judicial reviews

In Chapter 3 we noted that the court records appeared to indicate that there were not large numbers of groundless applications for judicial review being lodged. Since there is a question mark over the appropriateness of the current rates of grant and refusal of legal aid applications, it is interesting separately to examine the outcome of legally aided cases. We have not been able to follow up the actual cases on which the legal aid data discussed above are based, as many of them fall outside the period for which we examined court records. However, we are able to give information on the cases in our court database which appear to have been legally aided. The figures for the calendar years 1992 and 1993 would, perhaps, be the most relevant in principle, although it is worth comparing those figures to the longer-term trend.

In Chapter 3 we analysed the outcome of petitions for judicial review. It is possible to break these figures down further and assess the outcomes of cases in which the petitioner was legally aided. It will be recalled that the following categories were treated as successful outcomes: (1) petitions granted in full; (2) petitions granted in part; (3) extra-judicial settlements noted in the records; (4) other cases where there was evidence from which a settlement favourable to the petitioner could be inferred.[54] In 1992, 53.5% of legally aided petitions (23) were finally resolved with some degree of succeess for the petitioner. If cases otherwise taken out of court (which are impossible to classify in terms of outcome) are excluded from the analysis, the rate of success is 60.5%. In 1993, rates of success appear to have dropped, with only 38.5% of all legally aided petitioners (20) being to some degree successful, rising to 41.7% if cases otherwise taken out of court are excluded. The 1993 figures are against the long-term trend, with the overall success rate for legally aided petitioners for 1988–93 being 45.4%(88), rising to 48.9% if cases otherwise taken out of court are excluded.

In fact, the real rate of success is higher because the figures for final outcomes are affected by the peculiar features of immigration cases. In the majority of these cases the petitioner's main object is to obtain interim relief, especially liberation from custody in the form of an order of the court, or an undertaking from the Crown. Often this is achieved, but the principal petition is eventually dismissed because the substantive issues have been resolved in other fora, or the

---

[54] See Tables 7 and 8 in Chapter 3, at pp 30, 31.

petitioner has ceased to prosecute his claim. This effect also helps to explain the apparent drop in the success rate in 1993 – the number and proportion of immigration cases increased substantially in that year. Over the period 1988–93, of 59 legally aided petitioners, 36 had the principal conclusion of the petition dismissed, and are not, therefore, included in the figures for successful outcomes above. Of these, 23 (39%) obtained interim relief. In 1993, immigration petitioners were a larger than usual proportion of legally aided petitioners – 16 out of 52. Eleven of these petitions were dismissed, but in five of these cases (45.5%), interim relief was obtained.

Overall, these figures indicate quite respectable success rates for legally aided petitioners, and would tend to rebut any suggestion that legal aid decision-making is insufficiently strict, allowing an excessive number of unmeritorious cases. What the figures do not do is reinforce the reverse hypothesis – that legal aid decision-making is too strict – although they are at least consistent with it.

Appropriateness of the reasonableness test in judicial review cases

As indicated above, the application of the reasonableness test does not appear to be a major obstacle to access to judicial review in numerical terms, with only 26 applications being refused solely on this ground in two years. However, the fact that any applications are refused solely on the ground that it would be unreasonable to fund them, raises issues of principle. Here, we echo the concern expressed by the English researchers that some aspects of the reasonableness test may be inappropriate in some judicial review cases. However, it must be stressed that, as we have no information on the specific considerations within the broad umbrella of reasonableness which have prompted refusal of legal aid applications in Scotland, we cannot say to what extent our concern over aspects of the reasonableness test reflect a problem in practice.

The most fundamental concern relates to the application of the private client analogy, which may prevent legal aid being granted where a private citizen is attempting to raise an action which is of interest to a wider public. Mrs McColl's attempt to interdict Strathclyde Regional Council from adding fluoride to the water supply is an obvious example.[55] Legal aid was granted in that case, but Lord Jauncey suggested that this may have been inappropriate.

It is not clear whether practice has changed as a result of Lord Jauncey's comments. In principle, however, it must be questioned whether the private client analogy is appropriately applied to judicial review cases. The function of judicial review is not simply to enforce individual rights and interests, but also to ensure that public authorities act in accordance with law. Situations will inevitably arise in which a large number of persons, and sometimes the whole public of an area, (or, indeed, of Scotland) have a similar interest in an issue, such as fluoridisa-

---
[55] *McColl v Strathclyde Regional Council* 1983 SLT 616.

tion of the water supply. Such situations will arise more often in relation to public authorities than in situations where all potential parties are private bodies or individuals, simply because of the nature of the statutory powers and duties of public authorities, many of which relate to the public as a whole, or to very broad classes of persons. If legal aid is not available, the public interest in the legality of public authority decision-making may not be upheld.

It is possible that individuals will pool their resources to pay for legal action, but this is likely to happen only in a limited number of cases. The likelihood of this happening diminishes as the number of persons affected broadens, the potential cost of litigation rises, and average level of financial resources of the section of the public affected drops. The importance of individuals being able to assert the interests of a wider public is reinforced by the current state of the law on title and interest to sue which, although not strictly applied in practice in many cases, does appear to rule out most actions by pressure groups on behalf of those whose interests they represent.

There is an argument, therefore, for applying a different reasonableness test to judicial review cases than that applying to cases generally. Given the apparently influential *dicta* in *McColl v Strathclyde Regional Council* this would probably require legislation rather than a change of practice.

Summary and conclusions

Our research into legal aid applications in judicial review cases indicates that the number of applications for legal aid for judicial review has increased by around one-third over a three-year period, from 176 to 237. The breakdown of applications into subject-matter reveals that, as with judicial review itself, demand for legal aid is heavily concentrated in particular subject areas, notably housing (including homelessness) and immigration control, but with applications for legal aid to review legal aid decisions also figuring prominently. Some other subjects within the broad field of welfare law, for example social security and prisoners' rights, appear to produce fewer legal aid applications than might be expected. There is a substantial gap between the number of petitions for judicial review in welfare law areas and the number of legal aid applications, which appears to be largely explained by the high proportion of legal aid applications which are refused. We can, therefore, state that the level of initial demand for judicial review in the welfare law area is much higher than a study of court records reveals.

Legal aid applications are not distributed evenly across the country, and the data appear to suggest that this is because the possibility of using judicial review in welfare law cases is underexploited in some geographical areas, rather than because there are fewer opportunities for review in those areas. The work of solicitors involved in judicial review tends to be concentrated in particular subject areas. We have established that, for solicitors involved in housing cases, there are great variations in the numbers of legal aid applications which they submit, with a relatively small number submitting legal aid applications with any degree of regularity. Most applications come from solicitors in private practice. One law centre submits large numbers of applications, but the others do not appear to do so. It seems reasonably clear that only a small minority of solicitors applying for legal aid for judicial review handle immigration cases. We cannot state whether frequency of application varies widely within that group, as it does for housing cases.

In the general run of cases, the decision-making process appears to be reasonably swift, and most solicitors appear to be satisfied with the manner in which the special urgency provisions are operated. It does not appear that, in general, delay in obtaining legal aid substantially interferes with access to the courts, although there are some cases which experience substantial delays, and there appears to be considerable potential for delay in the processing of applications for legal aid for judicial review of Board decisions.

The most intriguing finding is the proportion of legal aid applications for the purpose of judicial review which are granted, which is very low in comparison to legal aid applications generally, and in comparison to legal aid applications for judicial review in England and Wales. This raises the potentially contentious issue of how this can be explained. It is not possible on the available evidence to confirm or deny any of the competing hypotheses but there is sufficient evidence to suggest that at least part of the explanation *may be* that legal aid decision-making in Scotland is too strict, and may be screening out meritorious applications. This issue requires further investigation. Whatever the explanation may be, it appears that there is not equal access to justice for litigants who might be eligible for legal aid on both sides of the Border.

Analysis of court records suggests that reasonably high success rates are achieved in legally aided cases, provided success is measured in terms of broadly favourable outcomes rather than the proportion of petitions which are formally granted.

Finally, there is cause for concern that the statutory criteria for awarding legal aid have the potential to rule out granting legal aid to individuals seeking to assert broad public interests. There is no actual evidence that this type of application is being made, let alone refused, although there appear to be no cases of this sort coming to court. However, the current state of the law appears, as a matter of principle, to be unsatisfactory.

Chapter 6
SURVEY OF SOLICITORS AND LAY ADVISERS

Introduction

The third stage of our research was a survey of the experiences and view of legal and lay advisers. The legal advisers included both solicitors and advocates. We had originally intended to survey persons who had petitioned for judicial review, but there was not sufficient time for this. In any event, it became apparent that there would be difficulties in making up the necessary sample. The survey of advisers was the major means by which we intended to examine the nature and impact of the factors which affect access to judicial review. This chapter is a discussion of those factors based on, but not limited to, the data derived from the survey.

Our initial hypothesis was that these factors would include:

(1) the extent of knowledge of, and expertise in applying, relevant law and procedure amongst solicitors and lay advisers;
(2) the availability of legal aid;
(3) perceptions of costs, legal aid availability, delays in the legal process and any other potential barriers to review;
(4) perceptions of the effectiveness of judicial review in giving the citizen a meaningful remedy against the administration.

As indicated in Chapter 5, the main concern was to investigate factors influencing access to review in the welfare law field, and the solicitors and advisers interviewed were chosen accordingly. We interviewed 21 solicitors and 13 lay advisers, all of whom had had some experience of conducting judicial review proceedings, or referring clients for legal advice and representation. Six of the solicitors concerned worked for law centres (five law centres in all), and the remainder were in private firms. We also interviewed five counsel, four of whom had considerable experience of representation on the welfare law side of judicial review. The lay advisers worked in citizens' advice bureaux, local authority welfare rights offices, other social work projects, Shelter housing aid centres, other specialist housing advice agencies, and the Immigrants Advisory Service. The solicitors were identified by us in a variety of ways, including prior knowledge of the researchers, information obtained from court records, and suggestions from both the Scottish Legal Aid Board and staff in lay advice agencies. The lay advisers were identified from the prior knowledge of the researchers and from suggestions made by solicitors.

We do not suggest that our sample of interviewees is representative of solicitors pursuing judicial review cases in the welfare law area in a strict statistical sense, but they do represent a substantial proportion of those solicitors who have been involved on the welfare law side of judicial review in the last three or four years.[1] It proved more difficult to build up the lay adviser sample. In part this was because there were fewer sources of information available to us. It may also be the case that there are more solicitors active on the welfare law side of judicial review than there are lay advisers referring cases to solicitors for action, but we cannot be sure of this. However, we consider that the numbers we have interviewed substantially reduce the probability that the views communicated to us in the course of the survey are atypical or eccentric, and we did succeed in covering the main distinct types of advice agency in our survey.

It seems reasonable to suppose that access to judicial review operates somewhat differently in the context of commercial cases and in the context of welfare law cases. Our main interest was in relation to welfare law cases, and the solicitors and advisers interviewed were chosen accordingly. We doubt whether there is a significant problem of access to judicial review for commercial clients, but that may be a matter that future research could cover.

Despite what may appear to be low absolute numbers in the sample, our survey covered solicitors and advisers working in a variety of locations and environments. The locations of their offices included Glasgow, Edinburgh, Aberdeen, Paisley, Ayr, Airdrie, Motherwell, Dunfermline and Stonehaven. However, some solicitors acted for clients outwith the areas where their offices were located. This meant that the casework of those interviewed derived from both urban and rural areas, and from regions having the bulk of Scotland's population. The main gaps in terms of the origins of cases were Highland Region, Borders Region, and Tayside and the Islands councils. We did not interview solicitors working in Central Region, but did interview one lay adviser referring cases in that area.

The lay advisers interviewed referred clients whose cases arose in Strathclyde, Grampian, Central and Lothian Regions. The gaps were, therefore, in coverage of advice services operating in Highland, Tayside, Fife, the Islands, and Borders. No advisers in Dumfries and Galloway were interviewed, but the solicitor sample included one who derived a significant caseload from that region.

---

[1] In Chapter 5, we indicated that the applications for legal aid had been made by 80 outlets in 1992/93 and 85 outlets in 1993/94, and a large proportion of these had been responsible for only one or two applications in those years.

6 SURVEY OF SOLICITORS AND LAY ADVISERS

We also interviewed five advocates, whose comments gave us some perspective on the comments made by solicitors and lay advisers in the course of the survey, as well as providing information relevant to the first two stages of the project.

The most obvious limitation of the method is that the survey comprised the views of those who were 'doing judicial review', rather than those who were not. Whilst our conclusions about access to review would be more securely based if the survey had included both groups, there were limitations of time and resources. We do not think that not surveying those inactive in judicial review seriously undermines our conclusions. Our assumption was that we would be able to find out something about why some advisers are undertaking judicial review work and why others are not, from our sample of the former, and this turned out to be the case. In addition, our conclusions are not based solely on the results of the survey. The other important evidence available to us was the data derived from court records, data supplied by the Scottish Legal Aid Board, and the impact study. We found, in so far as the interview data from the adviser survey were inconclusive on some issues, that when taken together with the data from the other sources the evidence tended to point in a particular direction. Finally, the conclusions were, in some cases, consistent with such previous research as touched on issues relevant to our project, and were generally intuitively plausible.

This part of the fieldwork was carried out between September 1994 and September 1995. The method adopted for this stage of the research was a semi-structured interview. The researchers based the interviews on schedules of questions for solicitors and lay advisers prepared in advance, but not adhered to rigidly. The majority of the interviews were tape-recorded. Both the specific findings of the survey, and broader conclusions about the factors affecting access to review, are described below.

Sources of solicitors' casework

Casework is defined to include not only cases which actually proceeded to a petition for judicial review, but also cases in which the solicitor had applied for legal aid for judicial review, or threatened judicial review, or otherwise carried out a significant amount of work on behalf of the client in a context in which the only formal remedy, in the absence of a favourable response from the other side, would be judicial review. All references to judicial review work or to caseload in this chapter should be construed accordingly. Our justification for doing so was the possibility that substantial numbers of potential judicial reviews might settle without the need for litigation.

The majority of solicitors in the sample reported at least some casework deriving from existing clients for whom they had acted on other matters, or from new clients making a direct approach to the solicitor on their own initiative. However, nearly half had never experienced this and derived their judicial review caseload solely from referrals from other agencies. Taking all the solicitors in the sample together, it is quite clear that the bulk of their caseload, which were primarily on the welfare law side of judicial review, was obtained by referral from lay advice agencies. The main sources of referral were Shelter and other specialist housing advice agencies, citizens' advice bureaux ('CAB'), local authority social work departments (both welfare rights officers and other social work staff), and the Immigrants Advisory Service ('IAS'). The pattern of agencies referring varies according to the subject-matter. As one would expect, IAS is a major source of referral in immigration control matters. Other advice agencies also refer cases to solicitors, but immigration control is one area in which a large proportion of the caseload is not derived from agency referral. A number of solicitors appear to derive a substantial number of clients from informal personal recommendations within ethnic minority communities.

Homelessness cases and other housing cases are referred to solicitors by social work staff, CAB, Shelter and other specialist advice agencies. Only a small proportion of cases came from solicitors' existing clients. Shelter operates three housing aid centres ('SHACs') directly in Glasgow, Edinburgh, and Aberdeen. In addition, there are four specialist housing advice agencies. Ayr Housing Aid Centre and Nithsdale Housing Aid Centre provide housing advice only. Lochaber CAB and Buchan Housing Aid Centre provide housing advice as part of broader functions. All four receive some funding and support from Shelter. Collectively, the specialist housing advice agencies are numerically the most important source of referral to solicitors for cases which proceed as far as a petition or a legal aid application, and are probably the most important source of referral for all casework.

Two recent developments are of interest in relation to the provision of housing advice. The first is that since late 1993, Shelter has operated the Scottish Housing Law Service ('SHLS') with Scottish Office funding.[2] The provision of the service is subcontracted to Legal Services Agency ('LSA'), a community-controlled law centre. In practice, all housing cases handled by the Glasgow and Edinburgh SHACs which require legal representation are referred to solicitors employed by LSA. The Aberdeen SHAC refers cases to local solicitors. The second development is the setting-up of the Scottish Homelessness Advisory Service ('SHAS'). This is a joint venture by Shelter and Citizens' Advice Scotland and is funded by Scottish Homes. It provides training in housing advice and a telephone consultancy service for CAB in order to improve the quality of advice given by them. Thus far, the service is operating in Tayside, Central and Fife Regions. It is intended to open further offices in Inverness and Glasgow, and the service will be fully operational in 1997/98.

SHLS has already produced a substantial caseload. It is too early to say what the effects of setting up SHAS will be.

Social security benefit cases are referred to solicitors primarily by welfare rights officers, but also by CAB and money advice centres. We encountered one

---
[2] See 1994 *SCOLAG* 98.

interesting example of internal referral in this area, namely Drumchapel Money Advice and Law Centre, where money advice workers are able to refer any case requiring judicial review to a solicitor employed by the same organisation. This has occurred in several cases.

It was not clear to us from the survey, or from other information, how education legislation or criminal injuries compensation cases find their way to solicitors. It may well be that in these areas the bulk of clients are persons for whom the solicitor has previously acted in other matters. We spoke to only one solicitor who had handled prisoners' rights cases; he had already represented some of those clients in other matters, whilst other cases resulted from recommendations from other prisoners. We suspect that this would be the case with most prisoners' rights cases. The remaining large category of cases was those against the Scottish Legal Aid Board. All of these arise from a refusal of, or other decisions relating to, legal aid applications, and in most of these cases the original application was not for judicial review, but for other types of proceedings, such as reparation or matrimonial matters. Here, as one would expect, the solicitor making the original application continued to represent the client in respect of the actual or threatened judicial review. Indeed, several solicitors had experience of judicial review only in this context.

Identifying cases as suitable for referral to solicitors

The role of lay advice agencies is crucial. They are clearly operating as gatekeepers in relation to judicial review. It appears that they are responsible for 'finding' the majority of cases for solicitors in the welfare law area. This places a heavy premium on the quality of advice given by lay advice agencies, in particular their ability to determine whether there might be a legal remedy for the client's grievance. The impression we have is that the ability of lay advisers to spot cases that are worth sending to solicitors as potential reviews is extremely variable. There may also be other factors at work which affect the propensity of advisers to refer cases to solicitors. Therefore, the level of activity on the welfare law side of judicial review is, to a large extent, determined by the advice agencies give, rather than by the extent of legal need.[3]

The evidence for this general conclusion is, first, the comments made by those who were interviewed. These comments were not unanimous. Indeed, solicitors were evenly divided on the issue of whether advisers are likely to miss cases which should be referred to solicitors. However, this result is not surprising in view of the fact that the solicitors interviewed were active in judicial

---

[3] As in Chapter 5, we are assuming that where a person has an arguable case that a public authority has acted unlawfully there is a need for legal advice and representation. For a discussion of the theoretical difficulties involved in making assumptions about the existence of legal need, see P Morris, R White, and R Lewis, *Social Needs and Legal Action* (Martin Robertson, 1973), especially pp 73–87.

review. We were likely to find that a fair proportion of these solicitors were dealing with advisers who were, as one solicitor put it, 'switched on to judicial review'. Therefore, this finding does not necessarily cast doubt on the conclusion suggested above. Other evidence reinforces the conclusion that only a small minority of the existing advice outlets are 'switched on' and referring cases to solicitors, and that many opportunities for review are thereby being missed.

The information derived from Court of Session and legal aid records which were discussed in some detail in Chapters 3 and 5, revealed that the geographical distribution of relevant legal work is extremely patchy, and it does not appear possible plausibly to explain this distribution by reference to objective factors such as population size or local authority policies. Further reinforcement for the conclusion above comes from our impact study. As Chapter 7 shows, the number of judicial reviews mounted against a local authority is a very uncertain indicator of the extent to which public authority decision-making complies with administrative law standards. It did not appear that the authorities most frequently reviewed were necessarily making more potentially reviewable decisions than other authorities which had largely escaped review.

It might be argued that this confluence of data showing a maldistribution of judicial review work indicates merely that there are problems with advising in general, without indicating whether such maldistribution lies on the side of lay advisers or solicitors. Is it possible that many cases are being referred to solicitors, who are then advising clients incorrectly that they have no remedy. Anyone who has experience of inter-professional discussions about welfare law will appreciate the sensitivity of this issue. It is commonplace to find solicitors blaming advisers for not sending them cases, and advisers blaming solicitors for not having the knowledge or the willingness to handle the cases. No doubt the low level of judicial review work in certain subject areas is caused by problems on both sides of the referral system. At this stage we are concerned to establish that, in the context of solicitors depending heavily on lay advice agencies for their caseload, non-referral by agencies, rather than failure to take advantage of referral on the part of solicitors, is the greater problem. However, it seems more likely to us that non-referral is the greater problem, because solicitors who were active in judicial review often depended heavily on lay advice agencies for their caseload, and because of certain other characteristics of the lay advice network, which will be discussed below.

The availability and quality of advice from lay agencies appears to vary according to subject-matter and geography. In general, housing (especially homelessness cases) is the subject area in which potential judicial reviews are most likely to be spotted and referred by lay advice agencies. It is worth considering three subject areas in detail.

Housing law

The specialist housing advice agencies (SHACs and independent housing aid centres) appear to perform much better on the whole than non-specialist agencies such as CAB. Solicitors taking referrals from the specialist agencies were confident of their ability to spot potential reviews and refer them when appropriate. Quite independently we gained the same positive impression from the specialist housing agencies who gave us interviews and supplied us with data.

It does not appear that non-specialist agencies are as successful at spotting and referring cases. One solicitor who specialised in housing law described his experience in this way:

> No, I don't think we have had any CAB referrals. If I was asked to generalise on my experience, I would say we get a number of referrals from the CAB, but I cannot think of a single judicial review type referral, and I suspect that is because the CAB will try to pursue the matter through the normal housing channels first of all, and, secondly, I suspect they do not know that many of the administrative decisions of councils are open to judicial review. ... I shouldn't be unfair to the referral agencies, because I know that some of the individual social workers do know that judicial review exists, but I would say that it appears to be a well kept secret amongst referral agencies.

Another solicitor with a substantial housing caseload said:

> I think the problem is that a lot of advice agencies do not have enough knowledge. That applies as much in Edinburgh where it would be even easier to review them than out of town, and this boils down to a lack of awareness of people in referral agencies who can actually do something.

Some of those working in lay advice agencies expressed similar doubts, and a representative of Shelter, the most prominent lay advice agency in the housing field, confirmed that in its view the quality of advice given on housing law in Scotland was extremely variable. Indeed, part of the reason for setting up SHAS (described above) was to fill perceived gaps in the provision of housing law advice.

There were positive as well as negative comments about the ability of generalist agencies to spot cases, but the evidence of the distribution of both litigation and legal aid applications tends to support the view that generalist agencies do not perform as well as specialist agencies. It might be thought that the comparatively low number of referrals from non-specialist agencies merely reflects the fact that the specialist agencies have cornered the market in housing advice. Although there is some evidence of referral from non-specialist to specialist agencies, this hypothesis appears unlikely. There are parts of the country not covered at all by specialist housing advice outlets, for example Borders Region. In addition, where specialist agencies have large catchment areas they find that, in practice, they have little or no casework arising in certain areas. Most of the caseload comes from areas within easy travelling distance of the office.

For outlying areas it appears that it is less likely either that clients will contact them on their own initiative or that they will be referred by another agency. Thus, the coverage in Scotland by specialist housing advice services is very uneven. There is, however, little correlation between the areas in which specialist agencies are absent or relatively inactive, and in which non-specialist agencies are active in making referrals to solicitors.

Immigration control

Immigration control presents a slightly different picture. We have already noted that a substantial proportion of the caseload is not derived from agency referral. The only specialist lay agency is the IAS, which has substantial expertise in immigration law and refers significant numbers of cases to solicitors. However, its only Scottish office is in Glasgow, and it is clear that a significant number of persons even within the Glasgow area go to non-specialist agencies for advice. We had some difficulty arranging interviews with immigration practitioners, but eventually secured interviews with three solicitors. One of these worked for the Ethnic Minority Law Centre, and had, in effect, a built-in network of referral through organisations represented on the management committee. The other two were in private practice. One of these appeared to obtain his clients through personal recommendations, and only the third appeared to derive part of his caseload from agency referral. We have very limited information, therefore, concerning referral from non-specialist agencies in immigration control matters.

The third solicitor's experience was that the work of non-specialist advice agencies was often not up to the same standard as that of the specialist agencies. He referred to two distinct problems with referral from lay agencies. One was the problem of non-referral of suitable cases:

> Quite often people come to us after they have been with a referral agency and we look at the file and they have been told by those in the referral agency that they have no case, but we decide that there is a case. The problem is that this is a fairly specialised area and without being overly critical of referral agencies, quite often the people who work in those agencies are not qualified themselves to ascertain and decide whether or not there is a legal issue which requires a judicial review.

The other problem was that the work carried out prior to an actual referral may well have done little or nothing to advance the client's case, and may even have made matters worse. The solicitor often received referrals which he thought should have been made at a much earlier stage. In these cases clients may have been wrongly advised by persons without sufficient knowledge either of immigration law or of the situations in which judicial review is appropriate. He considered that, had an early referral to him been made, a favourable resolution of the client's case could have been achieved, and at an earlier stage.

Social security law

The third area which merits comment is social security law. If it were a general rule that specialist advice agencies are more successful at identifying potential

6 SURVEY OF SOLICITORS AND LAY ADVISERS

judicial reviews than non-specialist agencies, then one might expect a large number of referrals to solicitors in this field, both because there are many opportunities for judicial review, and because this is a field well-served by specialist agencies. In addition to the large number of welfare rights officers employed by Scottish Regional and Islands Councils, there are numerous money advice centres and other projects offering benefit advice. Social security advice is also, in practice, one of the principal functions of the CAB which, although generalist advisers, thus have the opportunity to build up expertise in the area. At first sight the statement that there are many opportunities for review may seem strange given the existence of statutory appellate structures. However, there are likely to be significant opportunities for judicial review in this area, notably in relation to housing benefit and the social fund, but also in relation to gaps in the appellate system for other benefits.[4]

However, both the absolute number of petitions in social security matters, and the number of legal aid applications is low.[5] These figures tend to raise an inference that potential reviews in the social security field are being missed either by referral agencies, or by solicitors not putting forward legal aid applications, and the information and opinions derived from our survey tended to support this inference.[6]

It appears that the involvement of lay agencies, including specialist agencies, in referring cases for review is extremely variable. We spoke to one solicitor who had a varied social security caseload which had included the following issues: delay in fixing social security appeal hearings, various housing benefit matters, arguably illegal deductions of social fund loans from other benefits (sequestrated clients), and decisions made under the DSS *ex gratia* compensation scheme. This solicitor had more than one source of referral, but had received several dozen relevant referrals from a single welfare rights officer. Most of these cases were settled without the need for court action and many did not require a civil legal aid application but were dealt with under the Legal Advice and Assistance Scheme. By contrast, most of the solicitors interviewed had received no referrals from welfare rights officers or other agencies in social security matters. Even those who had handled social security cases could not approach the volume of work carried out by this solicitor. However, his caseload did not appear to depend on peculiar local features. The solicitor was a Glasgow

---

[4] *Ward, Petitioner* (unreported) 28 July 1995 (Court of Session) provides an example. The petitioner had obtained a favourable decision in an appeal to a social security appeal tribunal. This was later set aside by a second tribunal under reg 11 of the Social Security (Adjudication) Regulations 1986. A decision to set aside cannot be appealed, but the court granted an application for judicial review of the second tribunal's decision.

[5] See Table 2 in Chapter 3 (petitions) and Table 4 in Chapter 4 (legal aid applications).

[6] It has been argued that social security claimants tend to suffer from 'appeal fatigue' in multi-level remedial systems. See R Sainsbury, 'Internal Review and the Weakening of Social Security Claimants' Rights of Appeal', in G Richardson and H Genn (eds) *Administrative Law and Government Action* (Oxford University Press, 1994). It is possible that such 'appeal fatigue' might be part of the explanation for the low number of judicial reviews. However, the clear impression we obtained from interviews was that the role of advisers was the crucial determinant of whether opportunities for review in this field were exploited.

solicitor, but although he had a reputation for this type of work, he had not 'cornered the market' in social security work in that city. His main source of referral worked in one of 23 area social work offices in the Glasgow sub-region of Strathclyde Region, and the target of most of the referrals was the DSS, a central government department.

Two solicitors (including the one just mentioned) were confident in the ability of lay advice agencies to spot cases suitable for referral. However, they appeared to confine their remarks to their experience of agencies with whom they were in regular contact. The other two solicitors who had been involved in judicial review in this field were convinced that many potential reviews were being missed. One (who had been a welfare rights officer for a number of years) commented:

> I think one problem is on the social security side. People tend to concentrate on threatening judicial review because of delay and they are hooked on that one. ... they got solicitors to bombard the benefits agency with that and later on they bombarded the Independent Tribunal Service with that – focusing on that as if it was the only thing you could review, and not fully understanding the capacity to challenge the social fund inspector's decisions – only 14 challenges out of hundreds.[7]
>
> Social fund inspectors are a prime target and there you have a situation where people in the welfare rights industry take cases to the social fund inspector and stop at that point. They don't look at the decision critically. They don't seek professional legal advice and they don't consider whether or not it is worth challenging it ... the two cases in Scotland[8] ... neither one of them came through the large welfare rights sections of local authorities. So I think there is a gap there. There does not seem to be an awareness or proper training.

The impression gained from talking to solicitors was reinforced by one welfare rights officer who had, himself, referred many cases for judicial review:

> I refer a lot of cases to solicitors as potential reviews, as do a number of my colleagues in other offices, but only a few lay advisers seem to do this. Those working in advice centres must be missing a lot of potential judicial reviews that could be referred to solicitors. Most of them would not have a clue what you were talking about if you mentioned judicial review. This is true both of generalist agencies such as CAB, and of specialist bodies such as local authority welfare rights units.

Reasons for non-referral

If we are correct in concluding that lay advice agencies do not appear to be operating as fully effective finders of judicial review cases for solicitors, it is

---

[7] The solicitor was referring to the number of judicial reviews against social fund inspectors' decisions which had been brought in the United Kingdom as a whole at the time of the interview. The information was presumably derived from annual reports of the Social Fund Commissioner.

[8] *Gray, Petitioner, Court of Session* (unreported) 11 March 1994; and *Mulvey v Secretary of State for Scotland 1995* SLT 1064. These cases related to refusal of a community care grant and unlawful deduction of social fund loans from benefit.

6 SURVEY OF SOLICITORS AND LAY ADVISERS

worth examining what the reasons might be. In the abstract, it seems rational to suppose that to operate successfully as referral agencies they would require:

(1) detailed knowledge of the relevant field of substantive law (*e.g.* homelessness, immigration control, or social security);

(2) understanding of the substantive principles of judicial review (*e.g.* illegality, abuse of discretion, fettering of discretion, unfair procedure);

(3) knowledge of when judicial review is or is not a *competent* process, for example whether the decision-maker is subject to judicial review at all, whether statutory remedies have been exhausted, etc;

(4) the ability to synthesise (1) (2) and (3) to work out when a case needs to be referred to a solicitor.

The third point raised the issue of whether lay advisers are aware that administrative decisions in general are subject to judicial review, and that judicial review is particularly relevant where decisions are not made subject to any form of statutory appeal. It also raises the issue of whether they are aware that the principle of exhaustion of remedies normally precludes a judicial review application where a statutory right of appeal exists.

Intuitively, it appears excessively optimistic, and imposing an unreasonable burden, to expect lay advice agencies to be able to satisfy all of the above requirements across all areas of administrative law. The task will be particularly difficult for generalist advice agencies, and most of all for the CAB. The CAB are numerically the most important advice agency for members of the public. They are expected to advise on queries arising across the whole range of public administration, and to do so primarily through the work of part-time unpaid volunteers.

Inevitably, one has doubts about the ability of such a structure to spot the majority of potential reviews in clients' queries. Generalist agencies will typically have advisers who have a good working knowledge of certain areas of law, but not others. This means that they may not be able to satisfy (1) above. They will certainly not be able to satisfy (2)–(4) above without appropriate training and information resources. It is worth noting that core training for CAB workers, which all must undergo before giving advice to the public, included, at the time the fieldwork was conducted, coverage of social security law and housing law, but not immigration law. It did not include any material *specifically* on judicial review. Judicial review was mentioned in the advice notes provided to all CAB by Citizens Advice Scotland. However, the treatment of judicial review in the version extant at the time the research was conducted appeared to us to be unhelpful, and unlikely to supply any gap in relation to (2)–(4) above left by the training. Thus, it appears unlikely that the general training provided to CAB, coupled with the advice notes, could, in fact, produce the necessary knowledge of judicial review.

There are other training opportunities available to CAB workers, for example open access courses on judicial review organised by non-CAB training providers. We do not know to what extent such opportunities are taken up. However, it is worth noting that funds for external training are very limited and both the amount of these resources and the policy for allocating them will vary from CAB to CAB. We interviewed one person who had had a full-time job as a community support officer assisting CAB workers in central Scotland. He commented that in his CAB, funds for external training tended to be spent on sending full-time staff rather than volunteers.

We suspect that in generalist advice agencies as a whole, there is a very limited understanding of the principles of judicial review, and of the circumstances in which judicial review, rather than any other remedy, is the appropriate remedy to seek, although there are pockets of expertise in certain geographical areas on particular subject-matters. This was emphasised by one visit to a CAB in Glasgow which was relatively prominent in referring cases to a law centre. We were baffled that we had been recommended to visit this CAB, as the figures for referrals were extremely low. It only became apparent at the end of the interview that they had not regarded homeless persons cases, which they regularly referred to the law centre, as being within the ambit of judicial review. In this case the clients were not prejudiced since they found their way to a solicitor, but the anecdote makes the point that the nature, scope and significance of judicial review can be hard to grasp.

Specialist advice agencies ought to have an easier task. They deal with a defined area of administrative law, and their staff thereby have the opportunity to specialise. In practice, they rely far more heavily on paid staff than do CAB. In the case of local authority welfare rights offices, and the specialist housing agencies, advice is given almost exclusively by paid staff. However, the existence of specialist agencies does not appear to guarantee that potential reviews will be spotted. We found that wherever there is a specialist housing advice agency, there are significant numbers of referrals to solicitors through that medium, but the same was not true of social security.

Improving referral

Assuming our initial hypothesis, that judicial review is being significantly underused in the welfare law area, is correct, the next question that arises is what might be done to improve the situation. In theory, access to judicial review might work well without the intervention of referral agencies, but this would require citizens to present themselves directly to solicitors. However, a considerably smaller proportion of cases find their way to solicitors in this way, as opposed to via agency referral, especially if one excludes judicial review of legal aid decisions.[9] We have not attempted to assess directly why people do not go to see solicitors, but solicitors' views based on their contacts with clients appear to

---

[9] As indicated in Chapter 5, in most of these cases the initial legal aid application was not for the purpose of funding a judicial review.

be relevant. Most solicitors interviewed thought that their clients knew little or nothing about judicial review as such when they came to see solicitors. They were obviously aware that they might have some form of legal remedy against administrative action, but since most of them came from referral agencies, they clearly did not initially think that they should be seeing a solicitor. Previous research on unmet legal need has suggested that citizens may simply fail to realise that their disputes with public authorities may have a legal remedy, whereas in other contexts the appropriateness of consulting a solicitor is taken for granted.[10] Whilst the categories of dispute which the citizen intuitively classifies as 'legal' clearly change over time, there is no reason to suppose the phenomenon of failure to recognise that the existence of a potential legal remedy which a solicitor might pursue is not still a significant one.

Therefore, whilst attention should be paid to the solicitor's side of the equation, it appears that the greatest scope for improving access to judicial review for the citizen lies in focusing on the role of the lay advice agencies, which may be sources of referral, as they are most often the first point of contact for the citizen. The most obvious solution would be greater provision of specialist advice agencies. Although we have seen that this is currently working better in some areas than in others, in principle it would seem easier to reproduce the desired qualities ((1)–(4) above) in a specialist agency. That is likely to be an expensive solution, and until the funding is available, a more pragmatic approach would be to investigate what could be done with the existing network of CAB and other generalist advice agencies. It seems clear that in relation to such agencies, the training and materials available in the past have not been adequate to ensure that they function as effective sources of referral. This comment is not meant as a criticism of CAB. Expectations of what they can do must take account of the breadth of their remit, and the limitations of their resources. Inevitably, some aspects of advice work will receive more priority than others, whether consciously or unconsciously.

To increase the possibility that generalist lay advisers are able to spot potential reviews, it would be necessary to construct both training programmes and literature that addressed the four points mentioned above. Individuals, in order to be effective advisers, would need to have access to both training and appropriate literature. Two recent initiatives are relevant to this discussion. The first is SHAS – the aims of which were discussed above. The second is Scottish Homes Homepoint strategy, which is part of their programme of improving the provision of housing advice, and is intended, in particular, to improve the literature available to housing advisers. It is not yet possible to say whether either of these developments have had an impact on the performance of referral agencies.

Improving the performance of advice agencies will not greatly improve access to review unless the target of referrals – solicitors – perform their role properly. Good work by referral agencies in spotting a potential review will be wasted if a

---

[10] B Abel-Smith, M Zander and R Brooke, *Legal Problems and the Citizen* (Heinemann, 1973)

solicitor incorrectly decides that it is not worth taking up the case, or subsequently mishandles it. Generally, where advice agencies in our sample had established regular contact with particular solicitors, they were reasonably satisfied with their performance in handling judicial review cases. However, some had experienced difficulty in setting up such contacts. This did not surprise us. Advice agencies have traditionally had concerns about solicitors' knowledge of and/or willingness to get involved in a number of areas of law, including those most important on the welfare law side of judicial review (*e.g.* housing, social security and immigration control). There are solicitors who are both expert and willing to act in all of these areas, but it is widely accepted that there are not enough of them, and that in some parts of the country there is clearly difficulty in finding solicitors who are willing and/or able to take on work in these areas. Paterson and Turner-Kerr's recent research on legal advice and assistance tends to confirm this,[11] and advice agencies have, for a long time, reported difficulties in finding suitable targets for referral.

We encountered one particularly striking example of this phenomenon in our survey. A CAB operating in central Scotland had taken active steps to encourage solicitors to get involved generally both in certain areas of substantive law and in judicial review. A questionnaire was sent to approximately 12 solicitors firms asking if they were interested in specified areas of law, including social security and housing law, and whether they were aware of judicial review. Initially, there was an encouraging response from five or six firms. The CAB arranged meetings with these firms and invited them to specify the kind of assistance they might need, for example in-house training provided to them by the CAB. At this stage the solicitors appeared to 'back off', to use our interviewees' phrase. A number of months after the exercise had been carried out it had produced no concrete results. The CAB, found that, in practice, only one local firm was able to accept referrals in judicial review matters.

A number of the solicitors we interviewed admitted that they had begun taking on judicial review work without any prior background of experience of judicial review itself, or, indeed, of the relevant substantive areas of law, and that they had had to pick it up as they were going along. To represent clients effectively, the solicitor must be able to meet the same four requirements as we outlined for advisers above. We will return to the issue of how solicitors acquire their knowledge of judicial review itself later. With regard to substantive law, the division of labour between solicitors and lay advisers is such that lay advisers will often be more expert in the substantive law than the solicitors to whom they do or might refer cases. This is especially true in social security and housing matters where there are well-established specialist agencies. In the course of our research, we encountered examples of how agencies can make life easier for solicitors. Two agencies in particular effectively 'laid things on a plate' for the solicitor by highlighting the relevant provisions of the legislation, any respect in

---

[11] See A Paterson and M Turner-Kerr, *Research Report on the Distribution of the Supply of Legal Aid In Scotland* (Scottish Legal Aid Board, 1994).

which the decision complained of was contrary to legislation, whether any of the substantive principles of judicial review had been contravened, and relevant caselaw. This is an obvious way of plugging the solicitor's knowledge gap. However, this practice of 'active referral' is not uniformly followed.

Clearly, it is unreasonable to expect local solicitors with generalist practices to combine up-to-date knowledge and understanding of not just the principles of judicial review, but also detailed substantive knowledge of a multiplicity of areas of public administration, in addition to maintaining a practice dealing with the traditional 'bread and butter' areas of court work, such as matrimonial law, reparation and criminal law. We commend this process of active referral as necessary and desirable cooperation between solicitors and lay advisers. The lay adviser's role cannot be confined merely to spotting cases and passing them on without comment. That will not provide adequate access to judicial review for citizens unless enough solicitors specialise in both judicial review and the relevant substantive areas of law. However, such specialisation, if it means paying less attention to traditional areas of business, may not be an economic proposition for the average local solicitor. This returns us to the problem of ensuring that lay advice agencies have the appropriate expertise for the task.

Casework profile

With one or two exceptions, the solicitors interviewed had a relatively small caseload. Only a handful had had more than three or four cases proceed as far as a petition for judicial review in the Court of Session. For one or two, the actual litigation caseload was very much the tip of the iceberg. One solicitor had had approximately 40 cases with the DSS, all of which were settled by correspondence. They covered a variety of specific topics, with the largest group relating to decisions under the *ex gratia* compensation scheme. However, for most solicitors there was not much more of the iceberg under water. The handful of actual judicial reviews they had conducted was a substantial fraction of their total relevant casework, *i.e.* there were only a few more potential reviews which settled without going to court. The majority dealt with judicial review primarily in respect of a particular area, such as homelessness or immigration control, with a few having a varied portfolio.

These comments do not apply to some of the Edinburgh firms who act as Court of Session agents for local solicitors. Other Edinburgh firms acted as solicitors in their own right and not merely as local agents. Where Edinburgh agents were acting in their own right they were usually dealing with cases arising locally, but in one case the solicitor appeared to receive a substantial number of homelessness referrals from the area of Nithsdale District Council.

We interviewed solicitors from five law centres. Given that their avowed purpose is the satisfaction of unmet legal need, one might have thought that law centres would be very much to the fore in judicial review. In fact, law centres in general have not been particularly prominent in judicial review, although most have had some involvement. Should we be disappointed by their performance? The answer is not clear. At the time the research was being conducted, two of the law centres were too new to have established a pattern of work, and we did not interview solicitors in those centres. A third law centre was primarily a legal resource centre, and did not do casework. We did, however, interview solicitors from all the law centres which did casework and had already established themselves by the time the research was underway. The function of one law centre was primarily to satisfy unmet legal need within ethnic minority communities and it derived its judicial review experience, therefore, primarily from immigration law. Three other local law centres' activities were restricted to a defined geographical area. Two of these had a significant judicial review caseload, one did not, although the latter dealt with housing and social security matters within its general caseload. In the case of all three, local factors having to do with the characteristics of the rented sector of the housing market, and the policies of the local authority might well have resulted in opportunities for judicial review in the housing field being few. It is not clear why the third law centre had no reviews or potential reviews of a social security nature.

The law centre with the largest caseload is the Legal Services Agency, which had a larger caseload than nearly all of the private sector firms interviewed. A number of special factors apply to the Legal Services Agency. Unlike the other law centres surveyed the Legal Services Agency is a national organisation and has offices in Edinburgh and Glasgow. It has by far the largest staff complement (at seven or eight solicitors during the period of the survey it was larger than many of the private firms interviewed), and the most varied portfolio of general casework. These circumstances appear to have given it a greater number and range of sources of referral than the other law centres, and the opportunity to develop a wider range of specialisations amongst its staff. The most important of the special factors is that Shelter has subcontracted to it the operation of the Shelter Scottish Housing Law Service (SHLS). This results in large numbers of referrals, particularly of homelessness cases, which come directly from two of the three SHACs, or indirectly from other sources through the SHACs. Between early 1994 and the time of writing, solicitors at the Legal Services Agency had lodged more than a dozen petitions for judicial review derived from SHLS referrals, primarily homelessness cases.

It would be going too far to say that this is a model which should be copied, but it does indicate how a confluence of factors can apparently increase the level of judicial review in a particular area. The relevant factors here are: the existence of a network of specialist lay advice agencies within which the function of advice-giving has been substantially professionalised; the existence of specialist solicitors who have expert knowledge both of the generalities of judicial review and the details of housing law; and a developed system of referral from the former to the latter which operates on a cooperative basis. In the case of the SHLS, cooperation is institutionalised as the Legal Services Agency is contractually bound to supply a given level of service to the SHACs. However, the three conditions – expertise on both sides and an effective link – can be replicated without such an institutional connection if the approach of solicitors and lay advisers is the right one. We saw examples of these conditions being replicated in the case of links between the third SHAC and local solicitors, and between one of the independent housing aid centres and its local solicitors.

Legal aid

Unsurprisingly, given the areas of law in which the solicitors interviewed practised, they routinely applied for legal aid in potential judicial review cases. In general, they would not proceed with a judicial review case without either obtaining legal aid or being put in funds privately. As indicated in Chapter 5, the success rate of applications for legal aid is surprisingly low. Solicitors tended, in the aggregate, to suggest that they had higher rates of success in obtaining legal aid than was apparent from the statistics supplied by the Scottish Legal Aid Board, and there was also considerable variation in the success rates reported by them. It should be noted that these responses were based on the recollection of their caseload rather than the careful scrutiny of their files. The majority, however, were disappointed with their success rate on initial application. We asked them for their impressions of legal aid decision-making, including its general fairness.

A substantial minority of solicitors appeared to be content with the quality of the Board's decision-making. However, a distinct majority of solicitors were critical (some extremely critical) of the Board's decision-making. This critical view was also supported by four of the advocates interviewed.[12] There appeared to be no clear correspondence between solicitors' rates of success in obtaining legal aid and satisfaction or disatisfaction with legal aid decision-making. The satisfied minority included persons who had had a large proportion (up to half) of their judicial review applications refused, and some of the critics had been relatively successful in obtaining legal aid. The general view of the critics was that it was excessively difficult to obtain legal aid, and this was due to deficiencies in the approach of the Board. However, several solicitors indicated that in their experience, defects in decision-making cut both ways, in that worthless applications were granted, as well as meritorious applications refused.

The major criticism was that the Board and/or its reporters appeared to have inadequate knowledge of the relevant areas of substantive law, and inadequate knowledge of the principles of judicial review. We noted in Chapter 5 that the majority of applications are sent to reporters (usually advocates) for decision, rather than being considered in-house. Many decisions were thought to be extremely difficult to understand given, what appeared to the solicitor, to be a very strong case. Most refusals tended to be on the grounds of lack of probable cause. We listened to a number of anecdotes concerning cases in which solicitors were convinced that they had probable cause. If accurate, these

---

[12] The fifth advocate had no experience of legally aided judicial reviews.

certainly give cause for concern about the decisions in question. A further criticism was that the Board was stubborn and reluctant to listen to reasoned argument as to why the original decision was wrong. Many of those questioned applied for a review after refusal automatically, or virtually automatically, and some reported a very high success rate in reviews of initial refusals.[13] In general, there appeared to be widespread lack of confidence amongst solicitors in the competence of the decision-making process, and this was echoed by some advocates. A number of the comments made to us are reproduced below. It is clear from these comments that many solicitors were not familiar with some of the working practices of the Board, in particular the division of labour between in-house staff and external reporters. It should be understood that we are reporting the *views* of the solicitors we interviewed. We did not attempt any further investigation of the cases in which they had submitted legal aid applications.

Critical views were expressed by solicitors working in all the main areas of welfare law. One solicitor who dealt with many social security cases commented:

> SLAB [Scottish Legal Aid Board] tend to knock back good cases. In many of the areas in which judicial review is used, for example housing benefit review boards. They are not *au fait* with the relevant law. ... the initial decision-making is not very good and their standards are not consistent.

This solicitor went on to give examples of refusal of legal aid for judicial review in two cases relating to proceedings of two housing benefit review boards. As he described them, the proceedings of the latter appeared to be plainly illegal. However, in both cases legal aid was initially refused only to be awarded after the solicitor invoked the legal aid review procedure. Another solicitor who had also dealt with a number of benefit cases said:

> It is a bit eccentric. I had one where I had to go to review [internal review]. There was a big battle because the [respondent] had put in objections as to jurisdiction saying that the case had to be heard in England so we had this long exchange of correspondence with SLAB and they ultimately agreed with us. In another one, it was granted and reached counsel before counsel spotted that the papers did not include a copy of the [housing benefit] review board's decision which I had neglected to send to SLAB, but they granted legal aid without any question.

A third solicitor cited an example where evidence had been accepted *ex parte* at a housing benefit review board – a clearly unlawful procedure – yet legal aid for judicial review of the decision had been refused on the basis that landlord had provided evidence that conflicted with the tenant's version of events. This solicitor commented:

> SLAB don't seem to consider applications on their merits. They seem to have some policy which they don't publish. ... I think the decision-making is poor. There is

---

[13] Board staff have informed us that in some cases the main reason for granting a review is that further documentation has been produced or that the grounds for judicial review have been more coherently addressed.

6 SURVEY OF SOLICITORS AND LAY ADVISERS

ignorance at two levels – both of judicial review principles and, more importantly, of the substantive law. I think it has to do with the way reporters are appointed.

Solicitors active in housing law made similar comments. One said:

I have the impression that the Scottish Legal Aid Board don't really understand judicial review. They seem to confine themselves to asking whether a local authority decision is *Wednesbury* unreasonable, rather than looking at all the possible grounds of review. ... I find the difficulty of getting decisions off the ground because of the near impossibility of getting legal aid very frustrating. ... I think SLAB are motivated by financial considerations in refusing legal aid cases.

Another solicitor, with a particularly large homelessness caseload, said:

I would say that the merits of the decisions are extremely poor. I have no axe to grind with legal aid generally, but in housing cases, they don't appear to have staff with enough knowledge of housing matters, apart from one or two to whom I have sought to refer things I have been unhappy with, and have sometimes obtained assistance.

This solicitor also contrasted his success rate in judicial review applications with that in other areas:

... legal aid application for criminal matters where the people don't deserve any consideration are granted legal aid. You can put in judicial review cases, and legal aid basically put themselves as judge and jury on these cases and actually make a decision on the merits, which is the grounds of most of the judicial review of legal aid cases which I have [a reference to applications for judcial review of a Board decision to refuse legal aid].

A third solicitor, also particularly active in the area of homelessness said:

There seems to be no rhyme nor reason to the decisions. ... I think there are more meritorious cases refused than the other way round. ... You can only assume that it is going to people who have no real expertise in the area, or no real knowledge of judicial review and housing law. That may well be wrong.

An immigration practitioner said:

Usually, if we put forward an application for legal aid we have already decided that it meets the legal aid merits test, and, if they refuse it, then of course there is a feeling of unfairness. I think in immigration cases it is such complicated area which is evolving all the time and it requires an understanding of European case law and, even practising in [name of city], I have to keep up to date with decisions in the English courts, and it is a complicated area of law. I don't think there is anyone at SLAB who has the necessary expertise to properly deal with immigration-related cases. That is my own opinion. I'm not saying they don't try to be fair, but I am saying that in this area it is fairly esoteric at times, and sometimes very fine points are important. In some cases where we have had difficulty getting legal aid it has been because there was a lack of knowledge or understanding on SLAB's part.

The advocates interviewed provided reinforcement of the general tenor of solicitors' comments. Their experiences were based on their involvement in judicial review cases. None of them had acted as a reporter to the Board in relation to applications for legal aid for judicial review. One advocate commented on the standard of decision-making:

> Very variable. I have had decisions from them that did not show any understanding of the principles of judicial review. ... They are not very informed. They are fair in the sense that they look more to the merits of the case – the way people who don't know about judicial review do – than the actual principles themselves; but, again, that is very variable according to the individuals doing it.

Another advocate expressed particularly strong criticism of the Board's decision-making:

> I am absolutely ruthless in saying their decision-making is not up to scratch. You have people who quote in simple formulae the basic principles of judicial review and think they have it all sorted, and they simply do not know what they are talking about. .... I think they are turning them down, then sending them to somebody who knows something. Even the reporters, I do think, are people who don't know about judicial review, so there is a lot more to be done, and it is wasting huge amounts of public money, because it is not just the publicly funded legal aid person who is losing out here. In so many cases, the respondents are effectively public money, e.g. district councils or government, and they are paying, for appearances in court, hundreds of thousands of pounds which could be demonstrated to be lost as a result of the inability of legal aid to make good decisions here.

It is interesting to note that several interviewees clearly thought that the board was applying the wrong criteria in making decisions. Some examples of this type of comment are given above. Another solicitor, not previously quoted said:

> There are times when they apply a more stringent test than perhaps is in accordance with the probable cause test. Sometimes they appear to be governed by financial considerations rather than juristic ones. Some of their decisions in my view are based on not 'has probable cause been shown' but 'will this case win if it goes to proof?'. That is not the test in the Act. But, having said that, I don't think you will get a Board solicitor to accept that that is their test.

Several solicitors suggested that the Board was applying a higher standard than probable cause, for example considering whether the petitioner would succeed in a proof of facts (see above) or whether the respondent's decision might be defensible on its general merits, rather than whether the applicant had properly averred reasons why the decision would be reviewable (*i.e.* misunderstanding the legality/merits distinction which is fundamental to review). A number of solicitors clearly thought that the potential cost of litigation loomed too large in decision-making, and some were concerned that there were unpublished policies or guidelines that governed whether legal aid was likely to be granted in certain types of case.

Where solicitors and advocates ventured comments on the criteria employed to make decisions they were drawing inferences largely from their knowledge of the cases, rather than relying on direct information about the decision-making process. The only direct evidence available to them are the written reasons given for decisions. Until recently, these were simply notifications of which of the statutory reasons had been relied on – probable cause, reasonableness or both. Subsequently, slightly fuller reasons have been given. However, as noted in Chapter 5, the reasons given for refusals are very brief, and solicitors claim not to find them helpful in working out what was wrong with their applications.

Most solicitors were reasonably satisfied with the speed of the decision-making process with regard to decisions to grant a full legal aid certificate. In general, they were also satisfied with the speed of award of emergency legal aid under regulation 18 of the Civil Legal Aid (Scotland) Regulations 1987 (SI 1987 No 381). Emergency legal aid would generally be granted immediately on the telephone where it was thought appropriate, although solicitors would have to follow this up immediately by sending form SU4. There did appear, however, to be a difference of experience in relation to the justification for treating a case as an emergency under regulation 18. Most solicitors were content with this aspect of emergency applications, but several housing practitioners reported that their experience was that the Board tended not to treat many homelessness cases as matters of urgency.

A number of solicitors preferred to obtain counsel's opinion before making a full civil legal aid application, and thought that this increased their chances of success in relation to the final applications. However, some solicitors also indicated that the Board was reluctant to grant sanction for an extension of legal advice and assistance to allow for counsel's opinion. The Board has independently confirmed to the researchers that it does not think that, in general, an extension of legal advice and assistance for counsel's opinion is appropriate – the solicitor ought to decide whether or not the client has a good case himself – but it is always open to the solicitor to show why an extension to obtain counsel's opinion would be appropriate in a particular case. A few solicitors indicated that they thought that this approach was inappropriate.

The most striking point relating to legal aid to emerge from our interviews is that a majority of those interviewed thought that the legal aid system was interfering with citizens' access to judicial review, in the sense that a substantial proportion of meritorious applications are refused. This is an interesting finding in its own right, but it also raises the question of whether solicitors' criticisms are well-founded. This issue was discussed in detail in Chapter 5. We need not repeat that discussion here, but it is worth repeating the statment that, whilst no definite view can be expressed, there may be a problem of access to justice, arising from an unduly strict application of the eligibility criteria.

Costs

We asked interviewees about the cost of litigation. It is difficult to obtain precise information about costs. The information gleaned from court records has already been summarised in Chapter 4. The possible costs vary enormously according to how long the process takes. It appears that even a routine case which proceeds to a full hearing would be likely to cost over £2,000 for petitioners' legal fees alone, and could cost considerably more. All other things being equal, the fact of restricting judicial review to the Court of Session tends to inflate the cost, as both local agents and Edinburgh agents are generally involved, in addition to counsel.[14] It is clear that a person who neither qualified for legal aid nor had an income well above average would be unlikely to be able to finance the costs of a judicial review application. Information obtained from court records tends to back up estimates of costs given to us by solicitors.

In the legal aid cases (most of those our interviewees were involved in) the possibility of an award of expenses against the client where the petition was unsuccessful did not appear to be a major deterrent to proceeding with judicial review. The usual practice of the court when expenses are granted against a legally aided person is to modify the expenses to nil.[15] Even where expenses are awarded, they are often not pursued. The likelihood of clients having to pay the other party's expenses is, therefore, extremely small, and clients are clearly advised of this.

Solicitors' opinions about the extent to which clients are put off either seeking advice or taking legal action varied. Some solicitors thought that clients may well be put off by worries about cost; others thought that clients, in general, did not worry. Some solicitors thought that clients might simply be reluctant to see a solicitor at all because of their perception of solicitors, but, again, the majority did not think that was the case. In general, our sample of solicitors did not think that worries about cost were actually preventing people from taking judicial reviews. However, these comments were clearly based on their experience of dealing with actual clients. The view, certainly, is that once the client is in the door, and provided he qualifies for legal aid, fears about costs can be assuaged. However, clearly, to establish that people were not put off seeking legal advice, one would have to investigate the views of those who have not seen a solicitor. We did not attempt to interview any such persons.

---

[14] Currently, an action in the sheriff court might well cost more than a judicial review, because ordinary procedure in the sheriff court is considerably more cumbersome than judicial review.
[15] See the Legal Aid (Scotland) Act 1986, s 18.

Settlement

In many cases where a judicial review petition is lodged, it does not proceed to a substantive hearing. It was apparent from our research into court records that many cases were settled after the petition was lodged but before the judge had made a final ruling on the case. This impression was confirmed by our interviews with solicitors. In the homelessness cases, for example, a number of local authorities are clearly tending to throw in the towel once litigation has commenced and provide accommodation, hence removing the basis of the petition. Generally speaking, such settlements have been viewed by solicitors as being reasonably favourable to clients. They do not admit to accepting settlements which are much less than the client might be legally entitled to.

As regards what influences respondents' decisions to settle, few solicitors had much to say. The grant of legal aid seemed to have a significant effect in some cases, but not in others. One or two commented on the propensity of local authorities not to take an 'economic' view of the situation, meaning that they are prepared to fight a case all the way and incur considerable expense, whereas other litigants might give up in order to avoid the cost of litigation even if they are not convinced of the merits of the petitioner's case. Two sorts of comparisons were made by solicitors. Certain public authorities were compared to private litigants, for example insurance companies; whereas the latter would generally consider the cost of litigation as a major factor in deciding whether to settle, some public authorities appeared to be fighting cases virtually automatically. The second comparison was amongst public authorities, with some clearly counting the cost, and others clearly not. This was not a simple divide between categories of public authority – there was no clear central–local divide. The Home Office is thought to be keen to fight cases despite the cost; the Department of Social Security, on the other hand, is not.

Procedures and remedies

In general, solicitors and counsel were reasonably positive about judicial review procedures. Most local agents commented on the ease of use and suggested that much could be left to the Edinburgh agent. In principle, most solicitors thought that the idea of allocation to nominated judges was a good idea because it allowed them to build up expertise. Most solicitors claim to be unable to express how well this was working from their own experiences. However, one or two solicitors did comment that they thought that it did make a difference when the judge allocated to a case was not a nominated judge, and that the 'un-nominated' judges' lack of expertise did show. It appears that oral evidence is rarely taken; affidavits or, indeed, a petition without affidavits being lodged, usually sufficed. This suggests that in most cases it is possible to dispose of the matter by legal argument, without dispute over the facts. Most solicitors were reasonably satisfied with the remedies available, but a significant minority expressed the view that judges ought to be able, in appropriate cases, to substitute a decision for that quashed. This comment is interesting, but the suggestion runs counter to the basic principles of judicial review, in particular the distinction between the limited scope of review (legality) and the broad scope of appeal (merits).

Counsel

Solicitors tended to think that the choice of counsel made a difference, although in this respect judicial review was not necessarily greatly different from other areas of law. There appeared to be more concern to find counsel who were well-versed in the relevant substantive area of law (*e.g.* immigration control) than concern over knowledge of general administrative law principles or judicial review procedure. Most solicitors thought that they could generally find the counsel they wanted, but one solicitor suggested that it was difficult to find an appropriate counsel, and that there was not a sufficient choice of counsel who were well-versed in certain substantive areas.

Outcomes

We asked solicitors how often their clients' petitions were granted, or a favourable settlement was otherwise achieved. We also asked whether clients usually get what they want from the administrative process. Our aim was to investigate the fact that when a decision is reduced on judicial review this does not mean that the client ultimately gets the benefit that they seek. It is possible for the decision to be retaken with the same result but for different reasons, and for the second decision to be difficult to challenge.

We found that a pessimistic view that public authorities would routinely reinstate decisions which had been quashed was not justified by the evidence. Equally, it would be wrong to conclude that, as a matter of course, a client who is granted a judicial review petition would get the ultimate benefit he seeks. It is clear that in some cases local authorities will retake an original decision with the same result. Equally, in other cases, a retaken decision will grant the complainer what he seeks. In any event, a significant proportion of cases resulted in settlement without a final decision of the court. Such a settlement generally indicates that the petitioner has obtained most of what he wants. This pattern of a substantial number of successful petitions resulting in the petitioner getting the benefit desired, but a significant number also resulting in the decision being reinstated, is, in fact, entirely consistent with the theory underlying judicial review.

Knowledge and training

A number of solicitors commented on the lack of instruction in judicial review during their pre-qualifying training. There is probably more teaching of such matters in Scottish law schools than there was 15 years ago, but we must bear in mind that a significant proportion of those interviewed had, in fact, qualified more than 15 years ago. Even today, some Scottish law schools include only a limited amount of administrative law in those subjects which are compulsory for the LLB, or for professional qualification. It appears that the Law Society's prescriptions for public law are not interpreted as requiring a separate course in adminstrative law.

Most of the solicitors had picked up their knowledge of judicial review as they went along. The same tended to be true of their knowledge of those substantive areas of law which are outwith solicitors' traditional areas of work, for example homelessness. Some solicitors indicated that they were heavily reliant on their referral agencies to point them in the right direction. A number had attended training courses on judicial review in recent years, but few mentioned attending training courses in the non-standard areas of substantive law. Library resources appear to be very variable with, at one extreme, practitioners with very few resources, and, at the other extreme, practitioners maintaining a substantial library. Judicial review potentially makes considerable demands on library resources, since the solicitor needs to have both general administrative law literature, and literature relevant to each of the substantive areas likely to give rise to judicial reviews in which he practices.

Other factors

We asked solicitors whether they could make any other comment about factors affecting the number and nature of judicial review cases in the courts, the availability of legal advice and representation for judicial review, and other relevant matters. Most solicitors had little to say, but a few commented that there was a general lack of public awareness of the possibility of challenging the decisions of public authorities, and, if this awareness increased, there might be far more cases.

Conclusions

It appears from this survey of legal and lay advisers, taken together with the rest of our research data, that the most important factors affecting access to judicial review are probably the way in which cases are 'found' for solicitors, and the availability of legal aid. As regards the former, referral networks appear not to be operating as well as they might, and many potential reviews are being missed. As regards the latter, there is cause for concern that the legal aid filter may be screening out too many cases, and this issue requires further investigation.

Chapter 7

THE IMPACT OF JUDICIAL REVIEW

Introduction

The fourth element of our research was a study of the impact of judicial review on public administration in the context of the homelessness legislation. There is little literature specifically addressed to the impact of judicial review; however, there have been two notable empirical studies. The first of these was an examination by Bridges *et al.* of the effects of judicial review, including the GLC's 'fair fares' litigation[1] on local government public transport policy and decision-making.[2] The second study was Sunkin and Le Sueur's examination[3] of the impact of judicial review on central government departments. Both of these studies provided us with valuable insights. Also of direct relevance is literature on the implementation of the homelessness legislation, notably two pieces of Scottish Office research and Loveland's detailed study of three local authorities, all of which are discussed below. The impact of judicial review was not covered in the parallel research projects into judicial review in England and Wales, and in Northern Ireland.

The principal reason for studying the impact of judicial review was to provide a more rounded account of the role of judicial review as a means of ensuring the legality of administrative action for the benefit of citizens. Ultimately, the most important test of review as a means of ensuring respect for legality for the benefit of citizens generally is the extent to which it shapes or influences the administrative process, in particular whether it makes it more likely that administrative decisions are routinely in accordance with the law. The other elements of our research did not tell us all we needed to know about the effects of judicial review, in particular the analysis of court records told us little about

---

[1] *Bromley LBC v Greater London Council* [1983] 1 AC 768.
[2] *Legality and Local Politics* (Gower, 1987).
[3] 'Can Government Control Judicial Review', 44 *Current Legal Problems* 161 (note 3 of which gives useful literature references).

how administrative decisions and actions are taken in the vast majority of cases which do not lead to applications for judicial review. The study of legal aid applications and the adviser survey, whilst broadening the focus of our inquiry, gave us only outsiders' perspectives on the administrative process. It seemed necessary, therefore, to examine the impact of judicial review inside public authorities.

Our research should not be regarded as a full-scale impact study. This was only one of four elements of our research, and we were constrained by the time and funding available. To the limitations of the research itself must be added the limitations of this publication. Space does not permit a full account of the findings or full discussion of the points arising from them. A more detailed account will be published at a later date.

We chose to examine the impact of judicial review in the context of one administrative function only – the operation of the homelessness legislation. It seemed sensible to concentrate on one function only, because the impact of judicial review is likely to vary according to the function under consideration, and to look at a number of different administrative functions would have multiplied the difficulties of understanding, and allowing for, the broader context or contexts which affect the way in which different functions are performed. Given the emphasis on the welfare law aspect of judicial review in the legal aid study and the adviser survey, we wanted to choose one of the welfare law areas for the impact study to increase the possibility that all elements of our research would reinforce each other. Given, also, the need to have sufficient numbers of judicial reviews on which to base an impact study, the choice was effectively narrowed to one between immigration control and homelessness. The latter was chosen for a variety of reasons, including the possibility of making interesting comparisons between the way different local authorities perform the same administrative function.

Defining and assessing impact

Researching the impact of judicial review presupposes that impact can be defined and assessed. In defining impact, we chose to make two distinctions which cut across each other: the first between the particular and the general effects of judicial review; and the second between the implementation of actual judicial reviews and action which precedes or pre-empts any possible judicial review. By 'particular effects' we mean effects relative to individual cases, for example the means chosen to satisfy a particular grievance following a threat to petition for judicial review. By 'general effects' we mean effects not tied to particular cases, such as changes in policy or practice. As for the second distinction, implementation refers to the action taken as a direct result of a petition for judicial review against a public authority, or other formal steps preparatory to review, such as an application for legal aid. Pre-emptive action is taken because of the possibility of judicial review in order to avert or decrease the possibility of judicial review. Pre-emptive action may, itself, be a reaction to being subject to

7 THE IMPACT OF JUDICIAL REVIEW

judicial review where the action taken following review is intended to prevent review in future. It may also be purely anticipatory where pre-emptive action occurs without judicial review or the threat of it having been experienced. Pre-emptive action includes both action taken consciously, such as a change of policy, and less-conscious processes, such as a change in the attitude of decision-makers, or in the way officials carry out their tasks.

The purpose of making these distinctions is not to construct a schematic representation of responses to judicial review; rather, it is to illustrate that there are a number of dimensions to the impact of judicial review. It is a complex rather than a simple concept.

We considered that impact, defined in this way, could actually be assessed. However, some dimensions of impact are harder to assess than others. Thus, it is comparatively easy to determine what action a public authority has taken in response to a successful petition for reduction of a decision *when reconsidering that decision*. It is harder to assess whether and how officials are influenced in making decisions by the possibility that their decisions may be subject to review. Conclusions about some dimensions of impact are, therefore, more tentative than others. In this chapter, we concentrate on the more easily discernible effects of judicial review.

A further complication in assessing impact is the necessity to consider administrative action in its context or contexts. Any particular phenomenon studied may be produced by a combination of factors of which judicial review may be the only one. It can be difficult to separate the effect of judicial review from that of other factors, for example changes in the financial or organisational constraints affecting decision-makers, or changes in the broader social environment affecting the performance of administrative functions.

This analysis of impact led us to frame a more detailed list of issues for inquiry in the course of studying the impact of judicial review on public administration. We considered that the issues for inquiry might include:

(1) whether any application for judicial review led to a change in the law, or in the guidance given by the Secretary of State to local authorities;

(2) whether any judicial review led to changes in, or reconsideration of, an existing local authority policy or criteria for making decisions;

(3) whether any judicial review led to changes in local authority practices or procedures, in particular the way in which cases are investigated, and the way in which decisions are presented or explained;

(4) whether there were any perceived effects on the *general* performance of functions other than those mentioned above, for example a tendency to engage in 'defensive administration';

(5) the extent to which decision-makers are aware of the availability and significance of judicial review, and whether the possibility of being subject to judicial review, as opposed to the experience of having been reviewed, had resulted in any of the effects noted above.

The preceding questions relate to the general rather than the specific effects of judicial review. Further questions arise in relation to the particular effects on individual grievances:

(6) What happens when a petitioner is successful against a public authority in a judicial review? What new decision or action, if any, is taken in relation to his grievance? By what procedure? Does the public authority take any related action which affects the petitioner?

Two local authorities were selected for study on the basis that both had been the subject of a substantial number of applications for judicial review in homelessness cases. The fieldwork was carried out between January and June 1995. The fieldwork consisted of interviews, scrutiny of case files, and analysis of other documents. We interviewed councillors, officials in the housing departments, officials in the legal departments, and local advice workers and solicitors. We looked at files relating to: (1) cases which had resulted in applications for judicial review; (2) cases in which solicitors had become involved but which had not proceeded as far as judicial review; and (3) ordinary applications for assistance under the homelessness legislation which had not led to any formal proceedings. Interviews and file inspections were carried out in two local housing offices in each authority. Other documents inspected included local authority housing plans, in-house practice manuals and training materials. We guaranteed anonymity to the authorities concerned, and have therefore omitted certain information which would otherwise identify them (and which may help to explain the omission of certain factual details, particularly in respect of individual cases).

Prior research on homelessness

Before describing the results of our research, it is worth summarising the findings of earlier research on homelessness. Duguid's survey of policy and practice in administering the homelessness legislation in Scottish local authorities,[4] which was carried out in 1987/88, suggested that many local authorities were not acting in a manner consistent with the legislation. To give one example, 13% of local authorities stated that they rarely or never treated accommodation which is both overcrowded and a danger to health as justifying a conclusion that an applicant was homeless, despite a clear legislative requirement to do so. A further 21% of authorities only accepted such accommodation as constituting homelessness sometimes, and 15% normally accepted such an application, but not always. A second example of apparent illegality was found in the approach to intentional homelessness. A local authority tenant evicted for rent arrears was treated as intentionally homeless by 42% of local authorities. This is not a jurisdictional error like the previous one, but appeared to indicate that the

---

[4] G Duguid, *Homelessness in Scotland: A Study of Policy and Practice* (Scottish Office CRU, 1990).

authorities concerned might unlawfully have fettered their discretion. Answers given to other questions also suggested that fettering of discretion was a common phenomenon.

Duguid's research related to a period more than two years after the introduction of the special procedure for judicial review, and the consequent increase in the number of judicial reviews in homelessness cases. Whatever the impact of judicial review in individual cases, Duguid's research can be considered as an indication that the existence and increased popularity of judicial review had not, by then, ensured respect for legality in homelessness decision-making. Indeed, it may be the case that failure to ensure the legality of decision-making was even more widespread than the research might have suggested. The results were based on a postal questionnaire, and there was no direct scrutiny of decision-making. It would be surprising if local authorities which appeared willing to admit (perhaps unwittingly) to apparently illegal approaches to homelessness decision-making at the policy level were able to ensure that decisions on individual applications were, in general, consistent with the legislation and the principles of judicial review.

In the summer of 1993, Evans *et al.* conducted research designed to examine the operation of the 1991 Code of Guidance on homelessness.[5] This research, therefore, had a narrower focus than Duguid's research, although some of the questions asked were similar to those asked by Duguid. The most interesting finding was that there appeared to have been a change of approach by many authorities on a number of issues including: (1) the acceptance of certain types of accommodation as constituting homelessness *per se*; (2) which groups of persons should be seen as vulnerable, 'for other special reasons' for the purposes of defining priority need; and (3) the investigation of domestic violence. The relevance of these findings for our purposes is that such changes of approach would tend to reduce the number of decisions which were unfavourable to applicants, which, in turn, would tend to reduce the potential demand for judicial review. However, we must be cautious in drawing inferences about the potential for judicial review from these findings. Like Duguid's research, they were based on a postal questionnaire, and there was no direct scrutiny of decision-making. It could not, therefore, be assessed whether the general run of decisions on individual applications was consistent with local authorities' stated policies.

Loveland's research in England and Wales[6] was a two-year empirical study conducted between 1989 and 1991 of the way in which three local authorities administered the homelessness legislation. The book provides much valuable information for those interested in the impact of judicial review on public administration. The following passage summarises Loveland's conclusions on the extent to which the administration of the homelessness function was carried out with due respect for legality:[7]

---
[5] R Evans *et. al.*, *The Code of Guidance on Homelessness in Scotland* (Scottish Office CRU, 1994).
[6] I Loveland, *Housing Homeless Persons* (Oxford University Press, 1995).
[7] *Ibid.*, p 268.

At the most basic level, it is evident that from the data already presented that all three authorities modelled their administrative behaviour according to their perception of the Act's requirements. 'Homelessness', 'priority need', 'intentionality', and 'local connection' were key players in each council's decision-making process (albeit they were frequently misunderstood in Midland and occasionally subvented in Eastern). But it is equally evident that it was only Western (but even there by no means invariably) which lent these basic slogans an explicit and sophisticated legal gloss. Eastern's administrative processes were pock-marked with arguably *ultra vires* decisions, while Midland's decision-making was riddled with overt illegality.

Despite this, the three authorities concerned had little experience of being on the receiving end of judicial review. Even where a judicial review occurred and suggested a need for action going beyond the individual case, for example a review of procedures, there was little evidence of this occurring, nor was there significant evidence of *anticipatory changes* – administrators reacting to the general body of caselaw by seeking ways to conform the administrative process to judicial requirements.[8] There was, therefore, already a significant body of research suggesting that it should not readily be assumed that the strict observance of legal requirements was a feature of the administration of homelessness legislation.

The legal framework

For those not familiar with the homelessness legislation, a brief summary of the legal framework may be helpful.[9] The legislation was originally enacted as the Housing Homeless Persons Act 1977 ('the 1977 Act'), a UK measure which was brought into force in England and Wales in December 1979, and in Scotland in April 1978. As a result of separate consolidations, the relevant legislation is now Part III of the Housing Act 1985 (for England and Wales) ('the 1985 Act'), and Part II of the Housing (Scotland) Act 1987 ('the 1987 Act'). Significant changes were made to the definition of homelessness by amendments made in 1986[10] as a reaction to the *Puhlhofer* decision,[11] and again (affecting Scotland only) in 1990.[12] In other respects, the legislation remains unchanged. The effect of the amendments has been that Scots law and English law differ slightly on the definition of homelessness and the precise terms of the duty to rehouse homeless persons, but not in other substantial respects.

At the time of writing, the government has announced its intention of bringing forward legislation during the 1995/96 session of Parliament, substantially reducing the duties of English local authorities towards the homeless. No such announcement has yet been made as regards Scottish local authorities.

---

[8] *Ibid.*, pp 280–281.
[9] PQ Watchman and P Robson, *Homelessness and the Law in Britain*, 2nd ed (The Planning Exchange, 1989) provides a good general acccount.
[10] Housing and Planning Act 1986, s 14; Housing (Scotland) Act 1986, s 21.
[11] *R v Hillingdon LBC, ex parte Puhlhofer* [1986] AC 484.
[12] Law Reform (Miscellaneous Provsions) (Scotland) Act 1990, s 65.

7 THE IMPACT OF JUDICIAL REVIEW

The four fundamental concepts of the legislation are: 'homelessness',[13] 'priority need',[14] 'intentional homelessness'[15] and 'local connection'.[16] The first three concepts determine whether and to what extent local authorities are obliged to assist persons applying for assistance. A legal duty to secure the availability of accommodation on an *indefinite*[17] basis is owed only to persons who are homeless, who have a priority need for accommodation, and who did not become homeless intentionally.[18] Where such a person is merely threatened with homelessness, the local authority has a duty to take reasonable steps to secure that accommodation does not cease to be available. A person who becomes homeless intentionally is only entitled to be found temporary accommodation and to be given advice and assistance to enable him to find accommodation for himself.[19]

Once it is established that a person is unintentionally homeless and has priority need, the local authority may satisfy its duty either by providing accommodation itself or by finding non-local authority accommodation for the applicant. The duty to rehouse may, in effect, be transferred to another authority when the conditions for referral are satisfied.[20] This is where the fourth concept, 'local connection' comes in. An application may only be referred if the applicant has no local connection with the authority to which he initially applied (the first authority), but does have such a connection with another local authority in the United Kingdom, provided that the applicant will not run the risk of domestic violence in the district of the second local authority. Provided the conditions for referral are satisfied, the transfer is entirely at the discretion of the first authority, and may not be refused by the second authority.

The foregoing provisions govern the administration of the homelessness function by a complex mix of rules and discretion. Local authorities have substantial discretion in decision-making on some aspects of the definition of homelessness (reasonableness of continued occupation), on priority need (especially vulnerability), on all the main elements of intentional homelessness, and both in applying the conditions for referral to another authority (local connection etc.) and deciding whether or not to refer an application. Since there is no statutory appeal or other statutory remedy provided, the only formal legal remedy is judicial review. As the foregoing indicates there is ample scope for the application of the principles of judicial review, in particular those relating to the abuse and retention of discretion.

There is a very large body of reported cases. Many turn on their own particular

---

[13] 1987 Act, s 24; 1985 Act, s 58.
[14] 1987 Act, s 25; 1985 Act, s 59.
[15] 1987 Act, s 26; 1985 Act, s 60.
[16] 1987 Act, s 27; 1985 Act, s 61.
[17] Previously, commentators spoke of a duty to provide permanent accommodation. However, *Awua v Brent LBC* [1995] All ER 493 confirms that this is not an appropriate way to describe the statutory duty.
[18] 1987 Act, s 31, 32; 1985 Act, s 65, 66.
[19] *Ibid.*
[20] 1987 Act, s 33; 1985 Act, s 67.

circumstances, but many others have refined our interpretation of the legislation. In theory, decision-makers should take account of this caselaw in arriving at decisions. Local authorities also have a legal obligation to have regard to the guidance given by the Secretaries of State.[21] The guidance covers all aspects of the legislation and is supposed to encourage consistency in its implementation. They must also consider, when disputes arise over the referral of applications, a non-statutory agreement amongst local authorities on this topic ('the referrals agreement').[22]

Decision-making is, therefore, a complex task for officials, even if the focus of enquiry is restricted to ensuring the legality of decisions. There are generally three sources of criteria for decision: the legislation, the caselaw and either the Code of Guidance or the referrals agreement. In particular authorities, there may also be internal policy guidelines which are intended to structure the discretion of that authority's officials. All these criteria must be applied in a manner consistent with the principles of judicial review. This presupposes that officials can distinguish between issues on which they are bound by strict rules and issues on which the legislation confers discretion, that they are aware of the legal status of different criteria for decision and the way in which they should be permitted to influence decisions, that they can understand how concepts of relevancy, propriety of purpose, reasonableness, and legitimate expectation apply to their decisions, and that they are able to apply non-statutory 'rules' and policies flexibly, (*i.e.* without unlawfully fettering their discretion). However, the research referred to already suggests that the goal of lawful decision-making is often not realised in practice.

Local Authority A

Local Authority A is a district council situated in the central belt of Scotland. It has over 100,000 inhabitants. Over half the population is concentrated in a single large town. The rest is distributed over a number of smaller towns and villages. Although the bulk of the population is concentrated in urban areas, most of the land surface is rural, as the council covers a large land area. Farming and forestry are major land uses, but the area also has a substantial and varied industrial base.

The housing tenure pattern is as follows: at the 1991 census, over 60% of households were owner-occupied (higher than the Scottish average); over 30% of households were rented from public sector landlords (including housing authorities); and considerably fewer than 10% of households were rented from private sector landlords (including tied accommodation). In terms of numbers,

---

[21] 1987 Act, s 37; 1985 Act, s 71. Separate Codes of Guidance have been made for the two jurisdictions. See *Code of Guidance – Scotland* (Scottish Office, 1990), and *Code of Guidance to the Homelessness Legislation* (DoE, 1991).

[22] *Agreement on Procedures for Referrals of the Homeless* (revised 1979). The terms of this have been adopted for Scotland by the Convention of Scottish Local Authorities ('COSLA').

this translated into over 13,000 local authority houses, and over 1000 other public sector rented houses in late 1994.

Control of the council has alternated between Labour and Conservative parties, with the latter in power since the 1992 elections. However, there is a high degree of consensus on the main issues of housing policy and administration, including the approach to homelessness. The councillors and senior and middle-ranking officials interviewed were in agreement that there had been a great improvement in the quality of performance of all the main aspects of the council's housing functions since approximately 1989. The catalysts for change appear to have been the involvement of different councillors in housing management, and the appointment of new staff, including a new head and deputy head of the housing service. Senior staff and councillors apparently shared both a dissatisfaction with the way things were done before 1988 and a strong desire for change. The following comment made by the Convenor of the Housing Committee reflects the consensus view. Having agreed that there had been a great improvement in delivery of the housing service, he said:

> ... I think the culture in the department was abysmal. It was secretive; it repelled tenants. It responded to councillors' whims. It failed to think through policy. It failed to document adequately and it treated people in ways the public sector is often accusing of treating its customers ... I think the personnel changes in the housing department coincided with the arrival of different councillors, and it was partly the administration at the time and partly me, because I have taken a very keen interest in housing from virtually the start, and I think we operate housing fairly consensually. I felt when Labour was in power that I had quite a bit of say on the improvement of policies ... A lot of it [the improvement] has to do with the officers who came in at that time, who had experience elsewhere and also were ambitious, and who *wanted* to do a good job.

It is worth describing the apparent degree of pressure on the availability of housing stock and its relationship to applications under the homelessness legislation. Over 700 households applied as homeless in 1993/94, and over 500 of these were assessed as homeless or potentially homeless, but in other recent years, the figure has been as high as 900. The ratio of applications to local authority housing is, therefore, in the region of 1: 15–17. According to the council there are around 3500 households on the waiting list, and approximately a further 1500 council tenants seeking transfers. The number of council houses which become available for allocation each year is 600–700. There are, therefore, more homeless applications accepted each year than there are houses available, although not all applicants accepted as homeless have a priority need for housing.

Local Authority A has decentralised housing administration. There are six local housing offices, each of which has responsibility for the main housing management functions in its area, including homelessness. At one time, the homelessness function had been centralised, but since 1989 the responsibility for dealing with homeless applications has lain with local offices. Local office staff are, in principle, generic rather than specialist, so that no local staff are designated as homeless persons officers. However, interviewing and investigating of most applications is carried out by a particular person in each local office, so that there is *de facto* specialisation. This person will generally be a relatively junior official on a clerical grade, whose work is supervised by an assistant manager, responsible for homelessness, general allocations, and certain estate management functions. It is effectively the assistant area manager who makes the decision on the application on the basis of the information presented by the clerical officer. However, in straightforward cases the clerical officer may suggest what disposal is appropriate and get authority to give an immediate verbal indication of the decision to the applicant, which will be followed by written confirmation. Technically, the decision on an application is made by the area manager, but in practice the area manager generally rubber-stamps the decision of the assistant area manager. In a few cases, the area manager would, however, scrutinise the suggested disposal more closely and occasionally change the decision from that originally suggested. Applicants are informed in writing of the decision, as the legislation requires. Since 1992, the council has used standard form letters. There are nine specimen letters printed in an appendix to the council's *Homelessness Guidance Manual*, each tailored to a different category of decision. It is intended that officials add in the specific reasons for the decision, for example why a person is being treated as intentionally homeless, rather than simply duplicating the wording of the specimen. The specimen letters are drafted in such as way that the decision letter should always indicate at which of the four 'hurdles' an unsuccessful applicant has fallen (not homeless, not in priority need, intentionally homeless, no local connection).

The role of the central housing team in initial decision-making is advisory. Two officials there, the Principal Housing Officer (PHO) and the Housing Policy Officer (HPO) have particular expertise in homelessness. They would only be consulted prior to a decision being taken if they felt unsure of what the decision should be. The local offices are also in regular contact with the local housing aid centre, and despite the latter's role as applicants' advocate, local offices will ask for their advice and opinion on difficult points. The legal service are almost never consulted for advice on points of law, and this has been the case for several years.

When an initial decision is unfavourable, the council gives the applicant a right of appeal automatically. In 1992, the council set up a Housing Appeals Board (HAB), the composition and procedures of which were modelled on those of the statutory housing benefit review boards. However, the initial experience of hearing homelessness appeals before the HAB was felt to be unsatisfactory, and the great majority of homelessness appeals have been subtracted from the HAB's jurisdiction. Now, homelessness appeals go to the HAB if they are regarded as raising only a question of council policy. If there is any question of entitlement to assistance under the legislation, the appeal is considered by either of the PHO or the HPO, which, in practice, means that nearly all appeals are considered by them.

An appeal will usually be generated by a letter from either a local solicitor acting for the applicant, or the housing aid centre, more usually the latter. The appeal is then a paper exercise: it is based on the file and the letter of appeal. It does not involve a hearing and would not normally require further investigation of the case. The appeal is a comprehensive reconsideration and could result in a decision being revised on an issue of law, fact, policy or discretion. A successful appeal does not necessarily result in formal overruling. The PHO or HPO may, instead, convince the area manager by argument that it would be appropriate to revise the decision. Therefore, where a decision is revised, the second decision letter might be sent to the applicant either by the PHO/HPO or by the area manager.

The local housing aid centre is an important element of the decision-making environment. The staff consists of a co-ordinator, who gives advice and representation, and an administrative worker. The centre receives funding from a variety of sources, including the district council. About 60% of its clients are apparently self-referrals. Other important sources of referral are the district council itself, the regional council social work department, local solicitors and voluntary agencies. In a 22-month period leading up to late January 1995, the housing aid centre dealt with over 200 homelessness cases. Approximately 25 cases had been pursued through the internal appeals process in this period, and approximately 60% of these had led to a successful outcome for the client. A further 10 cases were referred to solicitors of which most had a successful outcome without the need for a petition for judicial review. Other referrals to solicitors did lead to petitions for judicial review. In a further group of cases (how many is not clear) the intervention of the housing aid centre has produced a favourable outcome for the client where the local office has revised its decision without going through the internal appeal process.

Judicial review in Authority A

Local Authority A was the respondent in 10 petitions for judicial review of its decisions on homeless applications in the three-year period from the beginning of 1992 to the end of 1994, more than any other Scottish local authority except Authority B. Before 1992, it had not been subject to a homelessness-related judicial review on any occasion. This is interesting considering that officials and councillors happily admitted that the general quality of delivery of the housing service was much poorer pre-1988 than it had been in recent years. It appears likely, therefore, that there was considerable unexploited potential for judicial review before 1992. The sudden explosion of interest in judicial review (six petitions lodged in 1992 alone) seems to have had two sources. One was the activity of the local housing aid centre in identifying suitable cases for review. The other is local solicitors who, although they received referrals from the housing aid centre, began taking up cases independently of it in 1992. Since late 1993, there has been a dropping off activity, with only one petition in the whole of 1994 and 1995.

The Authority's manner of dealing with these judicial reviews was somewhat unusual in that the legal department had virtually no involvement. In the first few judicial reviews the legal department had been involved in the usual way, as a channel of communication between Edinburgh agents and the housing service. Since then, the housing department has invariably dealt directly with Edinburgh agents. Nor was the legal department involved prior to lodging the petition. Solicitors' letters threatening to seek judicial review were sent direct to the housing department. Thus, the decision to adhere to an earlier decision which was likely to provoke a judicial review and all decisions about the conduct of proceedings were taken by the housing department. Once a petition had been lodged, the department had the benefit of the advice of counsel and Edinburgh agents. Before the lodging of the petition no legal advice was taken from outside the department.

Housing officials had chosen to bypass the legal department because they thought that they had greater expertise in the area of homelessness than the legal department. This was symptomatic of a wider clash of expectations. The legal service thought that it was offering an adequate service to all departments: the housing service was seriously dissatisfied with the nature of the service offered to it on housing law in general.

The housing department has a relatively robust and combative approach to judicial review proceedings. Although it frequently revised decisions through the internal appeal procedure, when a decision had been confirmed through this procedure, its initial reaction was always to defend judicial review proceedings. It appeared that its confidence in its decisions was not in any way shaken by receipt of a petition for review. Some petitions were fought to a conclusion. Where the council settled, this would not occur until the point where counsel advised that defeat was inevitable. Cost appeared not to be a consideration; indeed, officials considered it inappropriate to concede a case they had a chance of winning, merely because that would cost the council less money. In addition, there appeared to be no cumulative effect. The fact that 10 petitions had been brought in three years, in the majority of which petitioners had been successful to some degree, appeared not to have undermined officials' confidence in the correctness of their decisions or the rationality of always defending proceedings. Indeed, officials were prepared to argue that one of the decisions of the court which had gone against them was wrongly decided.

Of the 10 petitions lodged, eight resulted in some measure of success for the petitioners in court, in the sense that either the petition was granted or the petition was dismissed on the basis that the council would reconsider its decision. In the ninth case, the petition was simply dismissed by the court after argument. In the tenth case, the petition had been raised before the petitioner's legal aid application was determined. After the legal aid application was refused, the petition was dismissed.

Most petitioners ultimately obtained council accommodation as a result of taking legal action, including the last two petitioners' mentioned whose cases had 'failed' in court. However, in one of the cases which had been settled, the petitioner obtained accommodation herself before the council's reconsideration of its decision was complete, and in one of the cases in which the petition was formally granted, the petitioner was not offered accommodation as she had found accommodation on her own. There was only one case in which, having reconsidered its decision, the council reinstated an adverse decision finding that the petitioner became homeless intentionally. Therefore, although the council, on occasion, is willing to follow a 'successful' petition for review with a further decision to refuse to provide permanent accommodation, petitioners normally did obtain accommodation as a result of a petition being granted or a settlement achieved in court.

As with all preceding stages of cases that resulted in litigation, the response to review was entirely the decision of the housing department. The council was ordained to provide accommodation in one case, and in another, although such an order was not made, the Lord Ordinary declared that it was bound to provide accommodation. In these cases, the council had no choice but to provide accommodation. In the remaining cases, it was required to reconsider its decision. In practice, this meant returning the case to the area office which had first decided. Officials at the centre did not seek to impose a fresh decision, although they did advise on the implications of the basis on which the judicial review had been disposed of. Most of the cases which were successful from the petitioner's point of view raised doubts about the legality of the particular decision, rather than the legality of council policy or procedures. However, two cases clearly raised such issues. In the first, the council had made a decision that the petitioner was intentionally homeless because of the circumstances of his dismissal from employment, which resulted in his losing tied accommodation. The decision was reduced for the reason that the information available to the council could not support findings that certain aspects of the statutory tests had been satisfied (whether there had been a deliberate act or omission, whether the applicant was aware that his conduct was likely to lose him his accommodation, and generally that no reasonable local authority could have reached the decision on the information available). However, the Lord Ordinary also suggested that any decision letter by a local authority founding on misconduct by an applicant (*i.e.* to indicate a deliberate act or omission for the purposes of making a finding of intentional homelessness) should describe in factual terms what the authority was satisfied the applicant had deliberately done or failed to do.

This was a specific judicial suggestion as to what should be included in a decision letter in certain kinds of intentional homelessness cases. It is not clear whether this had any impact on the way decision letters were drafted. The PHO and HPO conceded that failure to put enough specification in decision letters (even when the information was on the file) had been a recurring fault in area offices, particularly in cases of intentional homelessness. On the other hand, they did say that they had, in any event, been encouraging area offices to put more detail in decision letters for some time, and their impression was that this was having some effect. There was, therefore, no specific instruction or briefing to staff or amendment of the homelessness manual following this particular judicial review. Our inspection of the files was inconclusive on this point. Certainly, we saw a number of letters in which the degree of specification could not be faulted, but it was hard to say whether there was a general trend towards improved specification in decision letters.

A later judicial review (the latest we looked at) had more far-reaching implications. The council had sought to refer the application of a young woman clearly in priority need to another local authority when she preferred to remain in Authority A. The decision was, in fact, based on a misinterpretation of the phrase 'family associations' in the definition of local connection. The council had relied on the explanation of local connection appearing in the inter-authority agreement on referrals.[23] This agreement had not been revised since 1979, and had been based on the original version of the 1977 Act, which did not define 'family associations'. The agreement, therefore, advised local authorities which family relationships should normally be considered, and also suggested that the relative in question had been resident in the area for at least five years, and that the applicant must express a wish to be near that relative. However, section 83 of the 1987 Act (which was apparently made applicable to the homelessness provisions at consolidation through a drafting oversight[24]) suggested a broader definition of 'family' than the referrals agreement, including, in addition to those mentioned there, grandparents, grandchildren, uncles, aunts, nephews and nieces. The decision to refer the petitioner's application was reduced on the basis that the wrong definition of 'family' had been employed to exclude consideration of one relative. Secondly, the council had fettered its discretion by applying the five-year residence guidance as if it were a rule in order to exclude another relative. More generally, the court thought that the council had misunderstood the way in which a local connection could be established, and wrongly required the petitioner to establish a family association *of the requisite quality* (*i.e.* more than a mere blood relationship to a local resident). The court thought that there was no need to explore the nature or quality of the relationship between the applicant and her family. It was enough that a relative within the class defined in section 83 lived in the area.

The court's third reason for granting the decision seems to be contrary to the reasoning in the leading local connection case, *R v Eastleigh Borough Council ex parte Betts* [1983] 2 AC 613. The second point appears not to be of wider significance, since the guidance on length of residence is lawful as long as it is treated as advisory only. However, the first point reveals a clear incompatibility between the referrals agreement and the Scottish legislation. In theory, this ought to have led to redrafting of that part of the agreement in so far as addressed to local authorities. In fact, the council wrote to the Convention of Scottish Local Authorities (COSLA) which had adopted the referral agreement explaining the implications of the decision. Several months later COSLA responded by

---

[23] *Op. cit.*, note 22.
[24] Section 83 originated in the legislation on sitting tenants' rights to buy local authority houses.

circulating to local authorities an advice note summarising the effect of the decision. However, COSLA has not, at the time of writing, attempted to redraft any provisions of the agreement.

The council itself was intending to observe the courts ruling on the meaning of section 83 in future cases.

Local Authority B

Local Authority B is also located in the central belt of Scotland, but in many respects its characteristic features differed from those of Authority A. The population exceeds 140,000, spread over a number of large and medium-sized towns. The area is urbanised to a much higher dgree than that of Authority A. The economic life of the area was formerly dominated by heavy industry, and has suffered a considerable loss of employment opportunities from the run-down of those industries. In general, the area is less affluent than Authority A.

The housing tenure pattern is also very different with, at the 1991 census, fewer than 35% of households in owner-occupation (well below the Scottish average), approaching 65% in the public rented sector (including housing associations), and around 2% in the private rented sector. In terms of numbers the local authority stock in late 1994 stood at over 30,000 houses, and the rest of the public rented sector combined at approximately 2000.

The political background in Authority B is different from that in Authority A. The council has been Labour-controlled for many years, and nearly three-quarters of the councillors are in the Labour group. There appeared to be no major divisions over housing policy within the Labour group. Councillors and senior officials appeared to share a general satisfaction with housing policy and management in general, and the progress of a very substantial capital programme in particular. The capital programme had concentrated spending on modernisation and improvement of housing in formerly 'difficult to let' areas. Councillors and senior officials appeared to agree that homelessness could be a politically sensitive issue. Clearly, tenants sometimes expressed opposition to the rehousing of certain persons in their area. Some officials also thought that, although councillors had no formal role in homelessness decisions or allocations generally, they were able to exert some informal pressure on local offices where they were aware of and opposed the rehousing of a particular family in their area. However, it was also felt that such pressure did not necessarily achieve its object.

According to the local authority there were over 12,000 households on the waiting list in late 1994, including over 5000 who were seeking transfer. More than 900 persons applied as homeless in 1993/94, and over 500 were assessed as homeless or potentially homeless. The best way to compare pressure on housing with Authority A is to look also at stock turnover. Authority A had 600–700 houses available for letting each year. There were therefore approximately eight persons on the waiting list, including those available for transfer, for every home available in a year, and more accepted as homeless in a year than there were houses to let. Authority B let over 2700 houses in 1993/94. With over 12,000 on the waiting list in late 1994 (including transfers) there appeared to be around five applicants on the waiting list for every house becoming available in that year, and more than five times as many houses available as there were homeless applications accepted.

Pressure on the availability of stock is, therefore greater in Authority A. It also appears that Authority A had a much larger proportion of homeless applicants relative to others on the waiting list. It accepted over 500 homeless applications in 1993/1994, as compared to about 5100 on the waiting list. Authority B had over 500 homeless applications, as compared to over 16,000 applications on the waiting list.

Authority B operates a decentralised housing service through six local offices. For several years up to decentralisation, the homelessness function was retained at housing headquarters. In 1992, the council decided to delegate administration of homeless persons applications to the local offices, although this change was phased in, office by office, over a period of time. Homeless applications are received by local offices, which are responsible for investigation and arriving at a preliminary decision. Within the local office, housing officers are generic (*i.e.* their duties are not restricted to particular aspects of the housing function). There is no *de facto* specialisation in investigating homelessness applications at housing officer level. The officers carry out the necessary investigations and bring the file to the assistant area manager for decision, although the housing officer will often make a recommendation. The initial decision will be made by the assistant area manager or the area manager, the relative roles of the two appearing to vary slightly in different local offices. In at least one office the appropriate disposal of homelessness cases is discussed at weekly meetings attended by both housing officers and managers. Once the manager and/or assistant manager has agreed the proposed decision, the file is sent to the Homeless Persons Officer (HomPO) at housing headquarters who writes and issues decision letters. In the majority of cases, the HomPO will agree with the decision proposed by the local office, but he estimated that he might send back as many as 30% for further inquiries or reconsideration. Where he does not agree, he explains why, and the local office usually accepts his decision. Where the local office is unwilling to accept the decision suggested by the HomPO, the case is referred to the Housing Department's Management Officer for decision. Authority B does not have a battery of style decision letters like those used in Authority A. Decision letters tend to be brief, but they do state which of the statutory reasons for rejecting an application for housing is the basis of an unfavourable decision (not homeless, intentionally homeless, etc.). There is generally also a brief further statement of why the relevant statutory concept applies, for example a decision letter stating that the applicant was intentionally homeless might go on to say that the applicant had given up settled accommodation at a specified address. In general, the further reasoning behind that conclusion would not be specified in the letter.

Decentralisation has not, therefore, gone as far in Authority B as in Authority

A, since, in Authority A, local offices do have authority to make decisions without reference to the centre. Because he issues the decision letter, the HomPO sees all files automatically. However, the local office may also phone him for advice on how a case should be dealt with before sending the file. On occasion, though infrequently, the local office will telephone the council's legal services section for pre-decision advice, rather than the HomPO. However, legal services would not be asked to approve a decision before it was issued.

No formal structure for hearing appeals against unfavourable decisions had been adopted, but in the last two or three years, the council appeared to have evolved a practice of reviewing decisions internally in some cases. The relative informality of this process can be gauged from the fact that no mention of appeal procedure is made in decision letters, and the fact that everyone we spoke to gave a different version of how it worked. It did appear to involve a review by a senior official, either the Management Officer or, if he had had some involvement in the original decision, the Housing Development Officer. At the minimum, the review would be based on a second look at the file, but further inquiries might also be undertaken. We were told that the introduction of a more formal appeals process on the model of a housing benefit review board is under consideration.

There was no local source of advice which had an equivalent degree of prominence to the housing aid centre in Authority A, but a regional social work department project providing advice and support to the homeless appeared to be a substantial source of referrals to solicitors. Most of the persons advised by the project were referred to it by the housing department, with the regional social work department providing most of the remainder.

Judicial review in Authority B

Authority B was the respondent in 10 petitions for judicial review of homelessness decisions in the period 1988–94. The two petitions received in 1988 were the first judicial review petitions of any kind against the council. Thereafter, there was a gap until 1992. The level of litigation increased dramatically, with seven petitions in 1992 and 1993. The tenth and last petition to date was lodged in 1994. There appears therefore to have been a tailing off of litigation in the last 18 months.

In contrast to Authority A, the legal service had a substantial involvement in the conduct of judicial review proceedings. It tended not to become involved until a petition had been served on the council or proceedings were imminent. Once the legal service became involved, it managed the case, corresponding with Edinburgh agents, and obtaining any necessary information from the housing department.

The legal service regularly found itself in the position of having less confidence in the soundness of the council's position than did the housing department. Therefore, although most petitions were actually settled, this tended not to occur until proceedings had been live for some time, and there had been a substantial exchange of correspondence with Edinburgh agents and some discussion of the issues in open court. One case which was sisted by the court for reconsideration was actually referred to the housing committee. Councillors backed the stance of the housing department. They took the view that the petition should be resisted to the end, and that they would not rehouse the petitioner unless forced to do so by order of court. However, some weeks later, and without further proceedings in court, the council did, in fact, reconsider the decision, and issued a fresh decision confirming the original finding of intentional homelessness. This was not subject to renewed challenge because the petitioner left for England.

In seven of the 10 cases, the petitioner had some degree of success in court in that the petition was granted or settled on the basis that the council would offer accommodation or at least reconsider the application. In the other three cases, the petition was dismissed: one following the refusal of legal aid, and the other two following a decision on the merits by the Lord Ordinary.

Most petitioners ultimately obtained some form of accommodation from the council as a result of taking legal action. One of the three whose petitions were refused was allocated a council house shortly after the conclusion of proceedings on a discretionary basis. Six of the seven 'successful' petitioners were allocated housing by the council, the remaining case being mentioned above, where reconsideration led to reinstatement of the original decision. However, there appears to have been more resistance to rehousing successful judicial review applicants than this brief summary suggests. In a number of cases the local offices to which the responsibility had been allocated appeared to have delayed allocating permanent accommodation because of reluctance to rehouse that particular petitioner, necessitating strongly worded reminders from either housing headquarters or the legal service.

There was a procedural difference from Authority A in the way that the council dealt with cases under review. Where reconsideration of a decision was required, that function was not delegated to the local offices. The fresh decision was the result of discussion between housing headquarters and the legal service. The only function of local offices was to allocate housing if the reconsideration resulted in a decision that accommodation should be offered.

In terms of the broader effects of judicial review, one case might be seen as something of a test case. The council had accepted the petitioner as homeless and agreed to rehouse her. The petition was founded on the argument that the duty to provide accommodation under section 31(2) had not been fulfilled because it was not reasonable to expect the petitioner to occupy it. The argument was rejected, and the opinion of the court appeared to suggest that a local authority could lawfully allocate accommodation to a person in satisfaction of the duty under section 31(2), even if it was likely that the person would then satisfy the homelessness test under section 24(2A). Section 24(2A) states that a person is homeless even if he has accommodation if it would not be reasonable for him to continue to occupy it. However, although potentially a test case, it is not clear whether the decision had had any effect on the subsequent practice of Authority B or, indeed, of Authority A which was aware of it. Nor can we say whether it has had an effect on the practice of other local authorities in allocating accommodation to homeless persons, since we did not examine the decision-making.

It appeared that reaction to judicial review by Authority B was not confined to reconsideration of specific decisions. The legal service, on several occasions, drew the conclusion that a particular judicial review revealed general deficiencies in the way in which decisions were taken. One notable example was the first of the crop of cases in 1992, in which the housing department received an application from a middle-aged man recently discharged from a mental hospital. He was advised that he could not be considered to be in priority need (on grounds of vulnerability) unless he produced medical certificates. A number of months passed without any final decision being made, and an offer of accommodation was not made until after a petition for judicial review had been lodged.

The head of the legal service then wrote to the Director of Housing suggesting that the case highlighted two deficiencies in the council's approach. The first was that the council appeared to put the onus on an applicant to prove that he was vulnerable in cases involving physical or mental illness, whereas the statutory provisions indicate that the council should make the enquiries necessary to establish whether the applicant is vulnerable. The second was that there had been undue delay in processing the application. By then, another petition for judicial review had been received and the head of the legal service suggested that there should be a review of the council's policies and procedures with respect to homeless persons, and suggested input to the review from the legal service. The Director of Housing responded by indicating that he shared the concern over the manner of treatment of certain homeless applications and that the issue would be raised with senior management in the housing department. This was the catalyst for the introduction of a programme of training consisting of seminars on homelessness given by legal staff for housing staff, which have been repeated at regular intervals. However, although training materials were distributed there was no equivalent of the extremely detailed homelessness manual adopted by Authority A.

It appears also that the practice of effectively requesting applicants to obtain the evidence necessary to prove vulnerability in cases of poor mental and physical health was abandoned. It appeared that efforts had been made to reduce the delay in processing cases, but we did not attempt to measure change in the speed of processing applications over time.

Both the investigation of cases and the drafting of decision letters were areas of concern. As explained above, the drafting of decision letters tended to be brief, albeit including in the case of referrals, a statement of which of the statutory 'hurdles' the applicant had fallen. From a close scrutiny of the files it appeared that in a number of the cases where the council had been forced to reconsider the petitioner's application, it might have been possible to ensure that the initial decision was unassailable. It appeared that in some cases relevant lines of inquiry had not been pursued, or it was unclear whether the decision-makers had addressed certain issues. Not only did decision letters lack the necessary detail, the 'missing' information sometimes could not be supplied by inspecting the file or interviewing housing staff. At the conclusion of one set of proceedings in late 1993, Edinburgh agents suggested that there were lessons be learnt with regard to decision letters.

Approximately 10 months later (late summer 1994), the judge in a further petition, although refusing to reduce a decision that the petitioner (whose problems included drug addiction) was homeless, commented adversely on the decision letter. The decision letter (issued in June 1993) had stated that:

> ... you do not have a priority need in terms of the Act. The reasons ... are as follows: you have no dependent children or other reason to suggest vulnerability.

The judge regarded this as the irreducible minimum that could properly have been given, and considered that where a statement of reasons was as uninformative as this one, it would tend to provoke suspicion and dissatisfaction on the applicant's part, and would be very likely to lead to litigation.

This judicial comment led the head of legal services to send a further memo to the Director of Housing suggesting that, since the decision letter was typical of the letters issued in all homeless cases, failure to have regard to the judge's comments would only leave the council open to challenge in future cases. The Director of Housing's response was that the legal department would be contacted with a view to arranging training for area housing managers, who would, in future, sign decision letters. This was not only a proposal for training, but a proposal for a change of policy. However, eight months later all decision letters were still being signed by the HomPO, who thought that he had insufficient time to write decision letters in the degree of depth that he would have liked, because he had to review the local office file, and write decision letters in nearly 1000 cases a year. From our scrutiny of ordinary case files, it appeared that in the spring of 1995, decision letters were no more detailed than they were previously.

Summary and conclusions

We can now summarise the impact of judicial review in these two local authorities. In both authorities the usual result of a successful petition for judicial review was that the applicant was offered a house, even where the court had not ordered the provision of accommodation. On occasion, however, both were prepared to reinstate a decision unfavourable to the petitioner. Not only is this consistent with the theory underlying judicial review, it also provides grounds for optimism that, at least in these two local authorities, despite the inherent limitations of judicial review, it often achieves tangible gains for applicants.

With regard to the general effects of judicial review, there are clear differences between the two authorities. Authority A had substantially changed the way in which it administered the homelessness legislation, and we considered that its view that the overall quality of homelessness decision-making had improved was justified. There were a number of particular features of the Authority's approach which might have been supposed to be reactions to judicial review, or attempts to pre-empt it – notably the training programme, the homelessness manual and the standard form decision letters. However, we were convinced of the Authority's claim that these measures were taken on their own merits, as part of a general programme of improving the delivery of housing service, and were not a reaction to, or prompted by anticipation of, judicial review. Where a specific decision of the court had broader implications these were not necessarily pursued – it was not clear whether any practical changed flowed from the decision in the tied accommodation case. On the other hand, the Authority immediately appreciated the significance of the local connection case which called into question the terms of the referrals agreement. This should have resulted in a redrafting of the referrals agreement, a change affecting Scotland as a whole. That has not yet occurred for reasons which are unclear.

In Authority B there had been a self-conscious attempt to learn lessons from the experience of judicial review. The legal service had, on several occasions, pointed out what appeared to be general deficiencies in policy and practice revealed by specific cases. Senior management in the housing department had accepted the legal department's analysis. The most obvious results of the stated desire for improvement were the provision of regular training in homelessness law, and an increased propensity of housing officials to ask the legal service for pre-decision advice; this latter effect was not particularly pronounced. However, it was not clear that the steps which had been taken had produced the desired results. The continuing brevity of decision letters was the clearest example of this. More generally, officials at the centre continued to be concerned that local office staff allowed a subjective element to creep into decision-making based on their perceptions of the worthiness of the applicant for assistance. They thought that the training had improved the approach of local offices, and the role of the HomPo provided a safeguard against unlawful decisions being issued. However, this clearly places a heavy onus on the central monitoring system given the HomPo's workload, and there must be concerns that some inappropriate disposals suggested by local offices will escape correction on central scrutiny. In this regard, the proposal to devolve the writing of decision letters to local offices, whilst it might cure the problem of the uninformative nature of these letters, may also create a problem with the substance of decisions.

The remaining question is whether any more general conclusions about the impact of judicial review can be drawn from our findings. A number of tentative conclusions might be offered of which the least tentative is that a great deal depends on context. One important aspect of context is that the frequency with which a local authority is subject to judicial review is not determined solely, and, perhaps, not even mainly, by the degree to which it makes legally indefensible decisions. That is certainly one factor, but the fact that the improvement of the quality of decision-making in Authority A coincided with an explosion in the use of judicial review suggests that it is not decisive. Nor is the frequency of review determined by the extent to which local authorities make decisions which are unfavourable to the interests of potential petitioners. The data derived from all four phases of our research suggest that a variety of factors influence the frequency with which a local authority is reviewed, of which the most important may well be the availability and quality of advice from both lay and legal sources, and the links between lawyers and lay advice agencies.

Where a local authority has actual experience of judicial review the effects are heavily influenced by the characteristics of that authority. Thus, it appeared that in Authority B attempts to learn lessons from judicial review were, to some extent, hampered by differences of perspective between officials in local offices and officials at housing headquarters. Our findings seem to support the familiar propositions that judicial review has a limited impact on public administration, and that, if the goal of administrative lawyers is to ensure that there is respect for legality in all bureaucratic decision-making, attention needs to be paid to the internal processes and administrative culture of public authorities. Our findings do not support the extreme view that judicial review is irrelevant. It can, in practice, provide concrete benefits for individual litigants even where, as is often the case, the legal effect of a judicial review is only to return the matter to the local authority for reconsideration. More generally, it can, as the experience of Authority B demonstrates, provide a strong incentive for administrative reform, even if it cannot guarantee that attempts to reform will be entirely successful.

Chapter 8

CONCLUSIONS

In our early chapters we examined the operation of the judicial review procedure in the Court of Session and reached what are, in general, very positive conclusions; the procedure has achieved the objectives of the reforms which introduced it through providing a relatively rapid and accessible means for challenging the legality of decisions, and has avoided the problems which have occurred in England after the earlier reforms there. Thus, there is no evidence of a serious overloading of the court through large numbers of weak petitions being brought; indeed, any problem is of under rather than overuse of judicial review in view of the relatively narrow range of subject-matter in the majority of petitions examined, and the limited number of solicitors originating judicial review cases. The issue of success rates was a complex one, but, taking into account the crucially important question of interim relief, we found that the success rates of petitions were high; indeed, noticeably higher than in England and Wales, where the role of interim relief in immigration cases is not so great. Moreover, the delay in the processing of cases is far lower than in England and, once correction is made for cases left inactively on the books by the parties, the Scottish speed of dealing with cases is very creditable, and urgent cases can be dealt with very quickly.

Our one finding which might suggest potential problems is the apparent rise in asylum petitions in the first three months of 1995; as this falls outside the period of our research we have been unable to study it fully. However, we would wish to make a more general point that if there is a future problem of overloading the court through an increase in judicial review petitions, the answer is to develop other procedures so that the use of judicial review becomes less necessary. We have suggested that this could be achieved by relatively minor changes to the licensing legislation, and another area for similar action might be that of homelessness. It could be argued that a rise in asylum cases does not support this conclusion, as new appeal rights were provided in the Asylum and Immigration Appeals Act 1993. However, evidence from our adviser survey has suggested that this has proved ineffective due to reluctance to give leave to appeal, and so judicial review has instead been used. This suggests a finding which we share with the English research: alternative appeal mechanisms must be accessible and effective in order to reduce the caseload in judicial review. What our research strongly suggests would *not* be an appropriate solution would be the introduction of a requirement of leave on the English model. Research south of the Border has suggested that such a requirement operates with considerable inconsistency, and our study of the cases suggest that it cannot be justified by the need to filter out large numbers of weak cases.

Indeed, we would suggest that the procedure has some important peculiarities which make English experience of little use as guidance to possible reform of the Scottish procedure. Most notably, the role of judicial review as a form of bail application through the grant of interim liberation in immigration cases has no southern counterpart, yet it serves an essential purpose in the Scottish legal system. As regards more specific points concerning the procedure, the decline in the proportion of cases heard by nominated judges may have led to some loss of specialisation, but it has not resulted in the sort of inconsistency found south of the Border, probably because of the fact that part-time judges are not used. The question of competence of judicial review appears to have caused few problems in practice; however, the issue of title and interest to sue needs some clarification both because of inconsistency in the existing caselaw and the radical changes which have occurred recently in the law relating to standing in England.

Overall, we are able to come to conclusions about the operation of judicial review in Scotland which are, perhaps, unusually positive for academic research. Indeed, we would go further and suggest that the key element in the procedure of maximising control by the judge may be a model for reform of other areas of civil procedure. It is interesting to note that this similar role for the judge in case management is a key recommendation of Lord Woolf's interim report on the civil justice system in England and Wales.[1]

Judicial review has, however, to be seen in a wider context of the factors which might limit the cases which reach the court. The first such factor was the grant and non-granting of legal aid, and here we found greater cause for concern. It should be stressed that the fact that we had no access to individual files prevented us from reaching definite conclusions either on the quality of legal aid decision-making or on the quality of applications submitted by solicitors. Nevertheless, we noted, first, the highly uneven geographical distribution of applications for legal aid for judicial review; more detailed examination of housing applications suggested that there was a considerable degree of concentration in a small number of solicitors' firms. This mirrors findings in the English research, and is further evidence that judicial review is underused. The speed of processing of applications for legal aid appeared to be satisfactory, but

---

[1] Lord Woolf, *Access to Justice – Interim Report to the Lord Chancellor on the Civil Justice System in England and Wales* (Lord Chancellor's Department, 1995).

8 CONCLUSIONS

the grant rate appeared to be very low; less than one-third of applications are granted initially, (less than two-fifths including successful reviews). This appears to be much lower than the proportion of successful applications in civil cases generally in Scotland, and much lower than the proportion of applications for legal aid granted in judicial review cases south of the Border. We cannot offer a single explanation for this low grant rate; it may be due to harsher standards being applied in legal aid decision-making in Scottish judicial review cases, or due to low quality applications being submitted by solicitors. We must note that there was extensive criticism of the quality of legal aid decision-making in judicial review cases from advisers we surveyed, including suggestions of a lack of expertise and inadequate reasons for decisions. Whatever the reasons for the low proportion of applications granted, it does give cause for concern; if judicial review is to develop its full potential it is essential that the filter represented by legal aid decisions does not operate in a way which is harsher than the decision-making of the court itself. Moreover, the lower grant rates in Scotland than in England raise problems of equality of access to justice on each side of the Border. We must emphasise, once again, that we have not been able to reach firm conclusions for the low grant rate, and that it does not necessarily form a reason for criticism of the staff of the Legal Aid Board, nor of the external reporters used. However, in view of the apparent problems we have described, we would urge that further research be carried out into possible explanations for our findings.

Discussion of legal aid as a gateway to judicial review leads directly to a further part of our research – the survey of solicitor and law advisers. We established clearly that the bulk of the judicial review caseload of our sample of advisers comes through referral by lay agencies to solicitors. This is, of course, less likely to be the case in areas such as commercial decisions outside the 'welfare' areas of specialism of our sample. Nevertheless, given the importance of 'welfare' cases in judicial review, this is an important finding, which suggests that maximising the effectiveness of judicial review will depend on ensuring that there are adequate lay advice agencies able to identify potential cases for referral. We found that the record of lay agencies in identifying such cases was variable, with some specialist agencies performing better than generalist agencies. The obvious solution is to propose the creation of more specialist advice agencies; however, this has resource implications. A less expensive, although less satisfactory, response would be to improve the quality of training and information available relating to judicial review in existing generalist advice agencies, such as the citizens' advice bureaux. As regards solicitors, we noted the particularly effective model of the Legal Services Agency, with a considerable degree of specialisation and strong links with referral agencies; this, however, is a model which cannot be replicated across the whole of the areas covered by judicial review. More generally, there were comments on the lack of instruction in judicial review in pre-qualification training for solicitors. Although there may have been some improvement more recently with more compulsory courses at undergraduate level, there is clearly a need for this to be further developed and for continuing education and training in judicial review matters.

The final part of our work was a study of the potential impact of judicial review on administration, both in its direct results where a petition was successful and, more indirectly, in shaping the administrative culture so that it is aware of the constraints on decision-making imposed by principles of legality. We must stress that at this stage we are only able to offer some preliminary conclusions on this matter; our main conclusion is that the relationship between judicial review and administrative behaviour is extremely complex. Two simplistic views about the impact of judicial review are clearly unfounded: first, the view that petitioners always get what they want as the ultimate outcome of the process; and, secondly, the view that judicial review is irrelevant to practice and that legal norms are not reflected in the final outcomes. What is striking, however, is that in both authorities which we studied, judicial review has taken on a new importance since 1992, confirming our earlier findings as to the relative success of the reformed procedure. Although the outcome in an individual case might not be what the petitioner was seeking, we have found some evidence that the use of judicial review contributed to more general improvements in administrative practice. However, this contribution was filtered through the culture of, and constraints on, the particular authority, making it difficult to predict such effects. We hope to research these matters further in the future.